BEGINNER GUITAR
THE ALL-IN-ONE GUIDE

The Missing Method
An imprint of
Tenterhook Books, LLC
Akron, Ohio

CHRISTIAN J. TRIOLA

Discover what you've been missing.

Copyright ©2018, 2020 Christian J. Triola, Amy Joy Triola
All Rights Reserved.

Except as permitted under the U.S. Copyright Act of 1976, no part of this publication may be reproduced, distributed, or transmitted, in whole or in part, in any form or by any means, or stored in any form of retrieval system, without prior written consent of the author.

Bulk sales and permissions inquiries can be directed to the author at info@themissingmethod.com.

Cover and Book Design by Amy Joy Triola, ©2018 Amy Joy Triola

The Missing Method™ for Guitar is an imprint of Tenterhook Books, LLC. The Missing Method name and logos are property of Tenterhook Books, LLC.

First Edition 2018, Tenterhook Books, LLC. Akron, Ohio.

Library of Congress Control Number: 2020911119

ISBN-13: 978-1953101006

Contents

About the Author v
Introduction 1
Access the Video Course & Audio Files 2

Unit 1: The Basics 3
Types of Guitars 4
Guitar Basics 6
Equipment 8
How to Tune Your Guitar 14
Basic Techniques 17
Right Hand Technique 19
Best Practices for Practicing 20
How to Take Care of Your Guitar 22

Unit 2: Playing Chords 23
Time 24
How to Read a Fretboard Diagram 25
The Fastest Way to Learn Chords 27
A Quick Lesson in Music Theory 28
Easy Chords to Get You Started 29
G Major and E Minor 30
Practicing G and Em 31
D7 Chord 33
C Major & A Minor 36
Review: G, Em, D7, C & Am 39
Using Common Chord Progressions 39
Eighth Note Strumming 43
3/4 Time 45
Rests 49
Ties 50

Unit 3: Reading Music 53
- The Elements of Reading Music 54
- Time 56
- Notes on the First String 58
- Notes on the Second String 61
- Notes on the Third String 64
- Notes on the Fourth String 68
- Notes on the Fifth String 72
- Notes on the Sixth String 76
- Introducing Accidentals 81

Unit 4: Tablature 87
- Tablature 88
- Reading TABS with Notation 91

Unit 5: Fingerstyle 95
- Fingerstyle: The Basics 96
- Travis Picking 104
- Block Chords and Double Stops 106

Unit 6: Power Chords 111
- Open Power Chords 112
- Root 6 Power Chords 114
- Root 5 Power Chords 117
- Combining Roots 120
- Three Note Power Chords 122
- Palm Muting 124

Unit 7: Basics of Popular Style 127
- Folk 128
- The Blues 130
- Rock 133

Country 135
Jazz 137
Classical 140

Unit 8: Ear Training 143

Ear Training 144
Interval Practice 146
Chords and Chord Progressions 153
Rhythm Training 159

Appendix 165

How to Change Your Strings 166
How to Practice with a Metronome 168
TAB Articulation Chart 170
Chord Reference Chart 173
Resources to Take Your Playing Further 174

About the Author

Over the past 20 years, Christian J. Triola has taught hundreds of students to play guitar and authored over two dozen popular guitar method books. He holds a Master's Degree in Education and a Bachelor's Degree in Music (Jazz Studies), and has played in a variety of bands in addition to his many solo performances.

What is The Missing Method?

The Missing Method™ for Guitar is an imprint of Tenterhook Books, LLC, owned and operated by Christian J. Triola and his wife, Amy Joy Triola. The imprint began in 2013 in an effort to bring method books that didn't exist to Christian's guitar students. Today, we have expanded that mission to create high quality instructional materials to inspire and empower guitar players around the world. The Missing Method now spans many series of guitar books, addressing topics from chords, to note reading, practice strategies, playing techniques and much more.

Learn more and join our growing community at TheMissingMethod.com.

Introduction

How this Book Works

When first learning how to play guitar, you are often faced with too many choices: do you learn to read music? Learn to read tablature? Strum chords first? And what about learning by ear? With this book, you will learn the basics of how to do all these things so you can discover for yourself what direction you want to take. Some will want to learn every approach, while others will simply want to strum along with their favorite songs. It's all up to you. There is no wrong way of learning guitar. You have to discover for yourself what works best for you for the style of music you want to play. And speaking of styles of music, this book also covers the basics of the most popular guitar styles, giving you a solid foundation from which to build.

With this book, you will be able to explore the world of guitar and decide for yourself what you want to be able to do with it.

What You Will Learn (And How to Learn It)

Each unit is designed to add to your overall knowledge of the guitar. Not only will you learn about note reading, chords, and TAB, but you'll also learn about guitar amps and other needed accessories, plus how to tune and maintain your guitar. Be sure to use the appendix as well. It contains important information on how to use a metronome effectively, tips for changing your strings, and much more, including a TAB chart showing you how to decipher some of the most common symbols used in much of the tablature you'll find in songbooks and online.

Overview & Recommended Approach

In Unit 1, you'll learn about the guitar and all the basic information you'll need to know about your instrument. Unit 2 starts you off by teaching you how to strum your guitar and read chord diagrams. In Unit 3, you'll learn the basics of reading music for the guitar, including how to read and play all the notes in open position. Unit 4 teaches you how to read tablature and gives you plenty of practice with it. Unit 5 delves into the world of fingerpicking. Unit 6 teaches you power chords, which are used in a variety of guitar music (but mostly rock). Unit 7 explores the basics of many different styles, from folk to classical and everything in between. Finally, in Unit 8 you'll be given the tools you need to understand how to play and learn songs by ear.

It is recommended that you read through (and practice) Units 1-4 first, and from there you can skip around to anything that interests you.

Access the Video Course & Audio Files

Included with your purchase are the free Beginner Guitar All-in-One Guide Essentials Course and audio files for each exercise and song. These can be accessed at https://themissingmethod.teachable.com/.

For your convenience, we've marked each topic with a video companion with the video icon.

One more thing . . .

If you enjoy this book and find it useful, please let us know by leaving a review on your preferred online retailer's website. Thank you!

Unit 1: The Basics

- Types of guitars
- Parts of the guitar
- Equipment
- How to tune your guitar
- Strumming
- Right hand technique

Types of Guitars

Acoustic

Acoustic Guitar Features
- Sound chamber
- Steel strings
- Pick guard
- Used primarily for playing rock, pop, country, bluegrass, and folk

Electric

Electric Guitar Features
- Pick-ups and Pick-up switch
- Tone and Volume Controls
- Sounds best when plugged in to an amp
- Used primarily for playing rock, pop, country, jazz, and blues

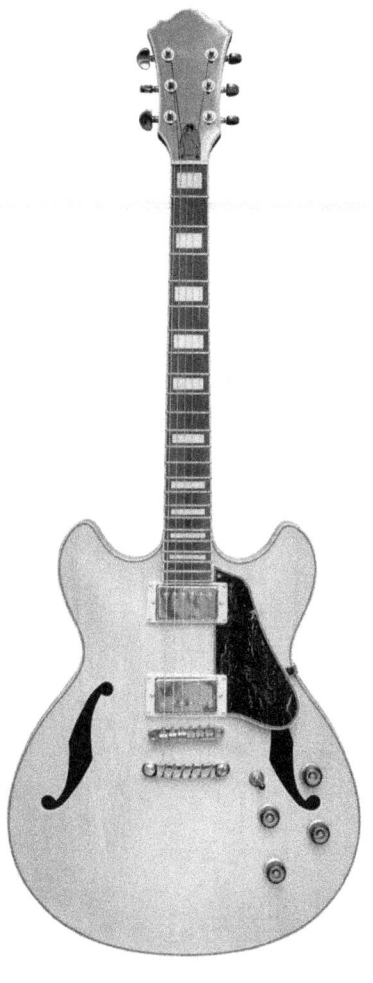

Hollowbody Electric

Hollowbody Electric Guitar Features

- Can be played plugged in or not
- Pick-ups and Pick-up switch
- Tone and Volume Controls
- Sound chamber
- F-holes (Similar to a violin)
- Used primarily for playing jazz, rockabilly, country, and blues

Nylon-string Acoustic (Classical)

Classical Guitar Features

- Wider Neck
- Nylon Strings
- Designed to be plucked with fingers rather than a pick
- Sound chamber
- Used primarily for playing classical music, traditional Spanish and Latin music

Guitar Basics

Parts of Guitars

 Video references: About Your Guitar & What to Look for When Buying a Guitar

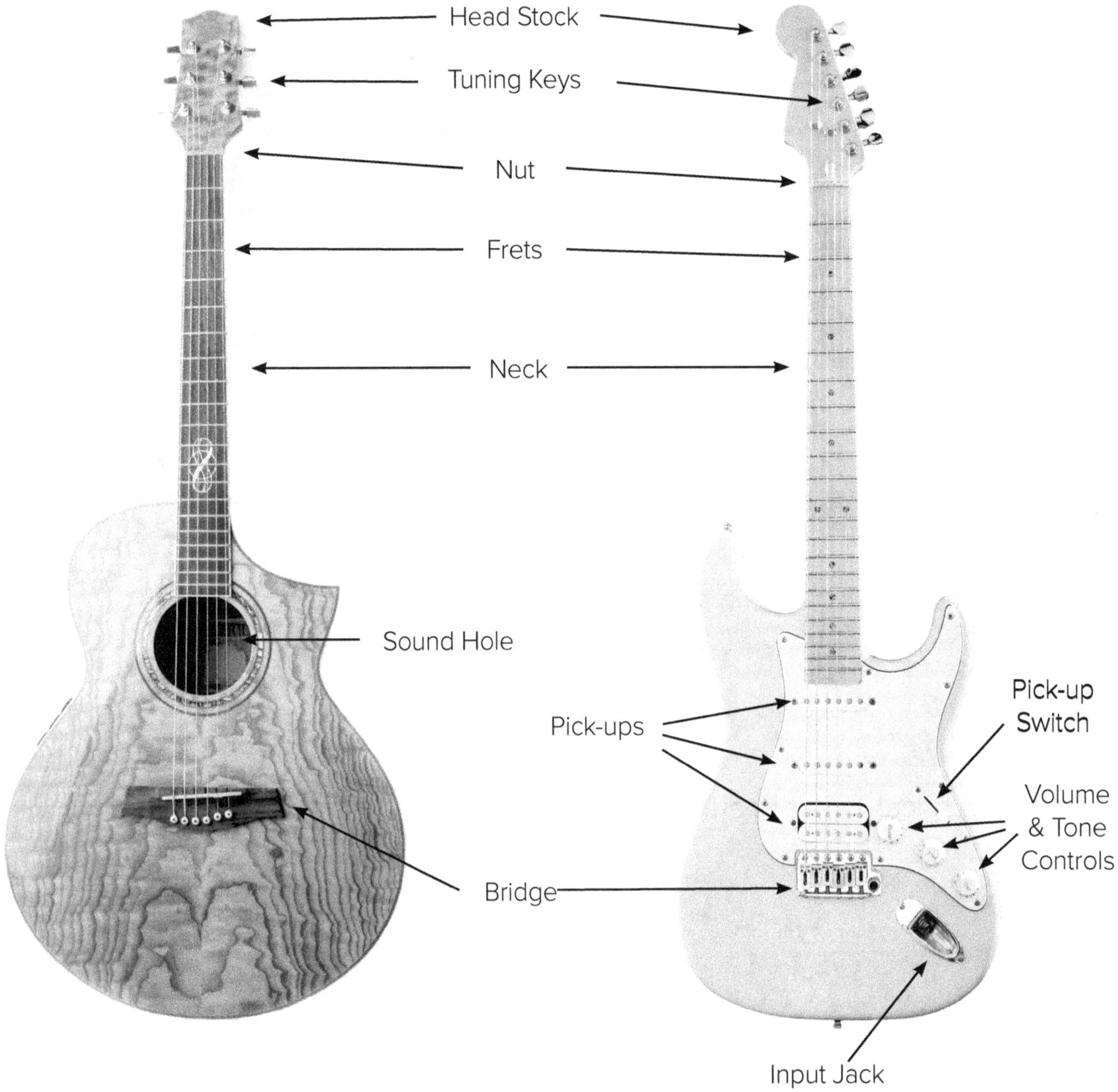

- Head Stock
- Tuning Keys
- Nut
- Frets
- Neck
- Sound Hole
- Pick-ups
- Pick-up Switch
- Volume & Tone Controls
- Bridge
- Input Jack

Action & Intonation

On all these different types of guitars there are things you'll want to look for that can make them sound great and easier to play.

First, is the **action**. Action refers to the distance between the string and the fretboard. The higher the action, the more effort you need to put in to get a note to sound. The lower the action, the easier it is to play. However, action that is too low can create fret buzz. High action can be beneficial because it produces a louder sound. However, most players prefer low action for ease of playability.

Second, is **intonation**. When a guitar is set up and constructed correctly, it will sound perfectly in tune no matter where you play on the neck. However, if you listen and find that higher notes sound somewhat out of tune as you move up the neck, then the instrument has bad intonation. On most electrics, this can be adjusted. On acoustics not so much. Though these adjustments can be made yourself, it is best to have a professional guitar tech do it for you at first to show you how it is done.

Equipment

Strings

Guitar strings come in all sorts of sizes and materials. Most strings are made from nickel, but not all. Some are made from nylon. When you first get a guitar, try to find out what size strings it came with. String sizes are shown on all guitar string packages. They are measured in millimeters and can range from as small as .008 to as thick as .054. For electric guitars, many players like sets of strings where the smallest string is .009 or .010. The thinner the string, the easier it is to bend, and the easier it is on your fingers. For acoustic guitars, .010 to .011 for the highest string is fairly typical.

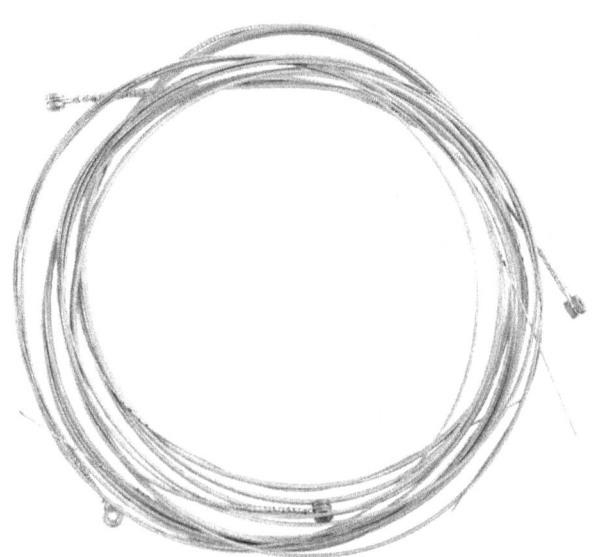

Example set of strings gauges (sizes):
  .009 (High E string, First String, thinnest)
  .011 (B string, Second String)
  .016 (G string, Third String)
  .024 (D string, Fourth String)
  .032 (A string, Fifth String)
  .042 (Low E string, Sixth String, thickest)

The exception for these measurements is the nylon strings for classical guitar. These are labeled as high-tension or medium-tension strings.

Also note that if you change the string size on your guitar, you will have to get the neck adjusted, since different string sizes create different amounts of tension on the neck. The heavier the string, the more tension on the neck.

Additionally, it is best to only use electric guitar strings on electric guitars and acoustic strings on acoustic guitars. I have had many students over the years who have tried to mix this up to see what it might sound like, but they have always been disappointed.

Picks

There are more types of picks than there are guitars. They come in all sorts of styles, sizes, shapes, colors, and materials, though most are plastic. Thin picks are great for playing fast, since they give easily but don't have a very strong attack. When strumming with a thin pick, it can sound "clicky" which is not a bad thing, it's just a different sound. Thick picks on the other hand, give you a solid attack on the strings. The best thing to do is get a few different types and experiment with them, to see which kind you like the sound of best.

Capos

A capo is a clamp that you place over your strings. These are used to help you change keys quickly. They allow you to use familiar or easy chord shapes in different areas of the neck in order to get higher sounding chords.

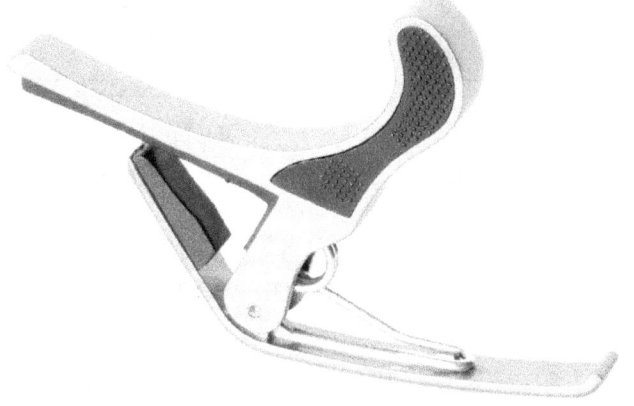

Amps

For electric guitars you have to have an amp. Amps come in all sorts of sizes, and each type of amp has its own distinct sound. (Some amps can even imitate the sounds of other amps). An amp can be measured by the size of its speakers and the number of watts it can put out. The higher the wattage, the louder the amp. If you just want to play at home, a 25-watt amp can be more than enough. But if you take that amp to a bar or coffee shop, you'll quickly see that you're going to need a louder amp, especially if you are playing with a drummer.

Amps break down into two main categories: tube amps and solid state. (There are hybrids that include both tube and solid state components.) Tube amps, as the name implies, use vacuum tube technology, and as a result, the tubes need to be replaced once they've worn out. For many musicians tube amps are well worth the hassle of replacing the tubes. The sound of these amps has a life to them that you simply can't get with a solid state amp. That said, solid state amps are highly convenient. (No parts to replace under normal conditions). And for many, they sound just as good as a tube amp. So listen to both if you can before you pick out your sound.

Once you've decided on a tube or solid state amp, you also have to consider whether or not you want an amp with built-in speakers (usually referred to as a combo amp) or without (where the amp and speakers are separate components). The advantage of separate components is that you can use one amp to power more than one set of speakers. These types of amps are great for live performances, but aren't too practical for at home use.

For beginners, I'd recommend a solid state 50-100 watt practice amp with built-in speakers. Many smaller amps come with lots of features including special sound effects like distortion and reverb, auxiliary inputs, and built-in tuners.

Cables

Guitar cables can be tricky. You can spend a lot of money on a cable that will die in a few months, or you can spend a few bucks on a cheap cable that will last for years. That said, most cables work well, and even though there are differences, just about any cable will do. They come in different lengths from a couple of feet to 50 or more feet. Keep in mind that the shorter the cable, the better the sound.

Effect Pedals

Also known as stompboxes, effect pedals are used with electric guitars to change or alter the sound of the guitar. Again there are too many different kinds to list here, but they can be broken down, more or less, into the following basic categories: distortion, overdrive, fuzz, wah-wah, volume, compression, reverb, delay, chorus, flanger, phasing, tremolo, equalizers, and loopers. There are many variations and other types, but these are just a few ways in which you can hone your own sound or discover how others developed theirs. The downside: these effects can get pricey, ranging from $50 up to $400 per pedal. You can also get effects processors which include several of these effects in one unit, but you don't have as much control over the overall tone of each sound. However, they can still be fun to play around with.

Pickups

All electric guitars have pickups, which are like microphones built into the guitar. They are placed in different sections of the body to pick up different sounds on the guitar. The pickup placed near the neck picks up warm tones and is aptly called the **neck pickup**. It is also often referred to as the "rhythm" pickup. The pickup near the bridge, known as the **bridge pickup**, picks up the brighter sounds, so it is often referred to as the "lead" or "treble" pickup. Some guitars have as many as three pickups and a five way switch to select combinations of pick up tones.

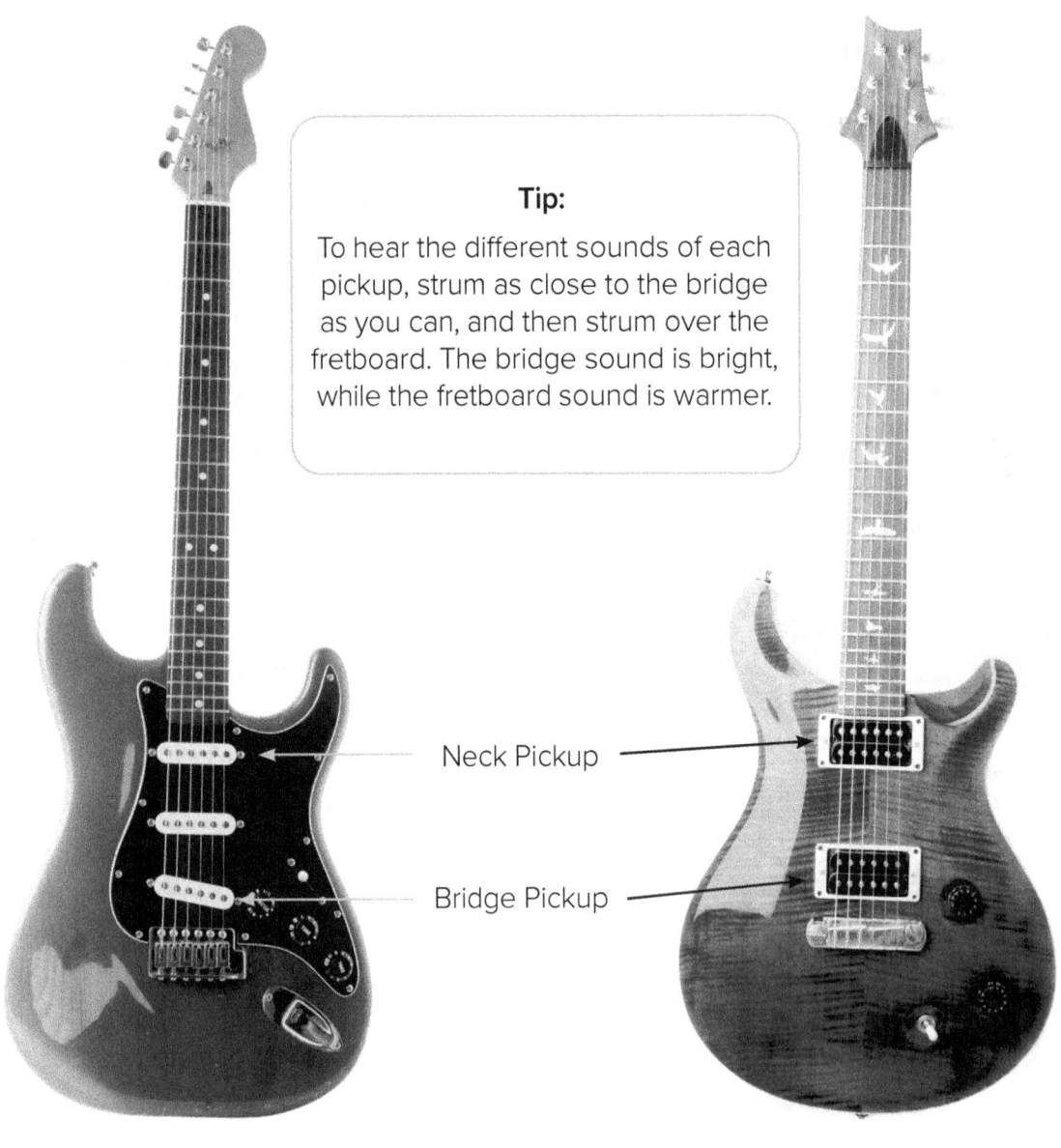

Tip:
To hear the different sounds of each pickup, strum as close to the bridge as you can, and then strum over the fretboard. The bridge sound is bright, while the fretboard sound is warmer.

Single vs Double Coil

Pickups basically consist of a magnet wound in wire. They pick up the vibration of strings, which is transmitted to your amp.

There are two basic types of pickups, each giving you a different sound to work with. The first, developed in the 1920s, was the **single-coil pickup**. These produce a crisp, bright tone. However, they can also produce a noisy humming sound in the amp.

Single Coil Pickups

The second type of pickup is called a **humbucker** or a **double-coil pickup**. This pickup was built in an attempt to cancel out the humming sound of the single-coil, and it worked. However, the resulting tone was warmer and darker than the single-coil sound, so today both types of pickups are used just as frequently.

Active vs Passive

Another classification of pickups is **active** and **passive**. The active pickup requires a battery while a passive pickup does not. Again, each one produces a different tone.

Double Coil Pickups

BASICS

 **How to Tune Your Guitar**

1 The first thing you need to know in order to tune the guitar is what notes to tune to. The chart below shows you the pitches of each string.

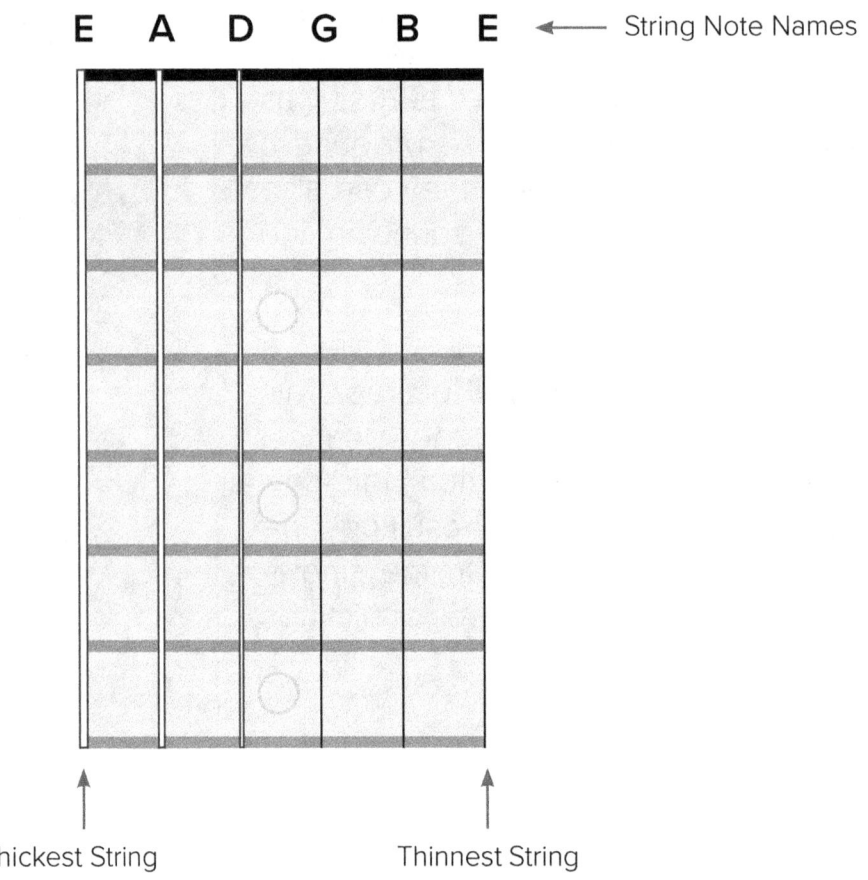

There are a couple of sayings that can help you remember the names of the strings, from thick to thin:

Eddie **A**te **D**ynamite, **G**ood **B**ye **E**ddie.

Or the less violent:

Every **A**mateur **D**oes **G**et **B**etter **E**ventually.

2 The second thing you should know is that tuning takes practice. It can be a little frustrating at first, but once you've done it a few times it gets easier and easier.

3 The third thing you need to know is that most of the time your guitar will only need slight adjustments. Once it's in tune, it will usually stay fairly close to tune most of the time. However, it is recommended that you check your tuning every time you pick up the guitar. Be sure to listen carefully to the sound of an in-tune guitar, so you become familiar with what it should sound like.

4 Now that you know this, we can begin tuning the guitar. There are several tuning methods. The best method is to buy a guitar tuner and learn how to use it. (You can find information on tuners on the next page.)

Typically, most tuners will show which note you are playing and then tell you whether or not the note is too low, too high, or in tune. Usually, a meter of some kind will display this information.

If the string is too low, you'll want to tighten the string. If the string is too high, you'll want to loosen it. Be sure to listen to the sound of the string as well. Your ear will help you figure out if you are going too far from the in-tune note.

 Guitar Tuners

Tuners come in all shapes and sizes. There are credit card sized tuners, apps, and clip-on tuners that attach to your guitar. The best apps for tuning include Pitchlab and GuitarTuna. There are many others that can work as well and most of them are free.

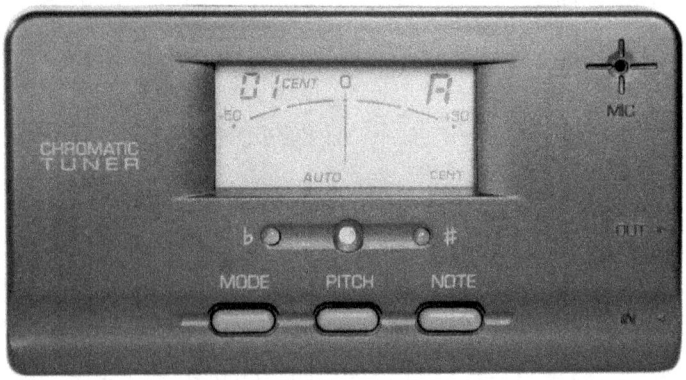

You can also search YouTube for lessons and suggestions on how to get your guitar in tune.

Another way you can tune the guitar is to use a reference pitch from an instrument that is already in tune. Most people use a piano, another in-tune guitar, or a pitch pipe to achieve this. In this case, you simply listen to the reference pitch and then match that pitch on your instrument. This can be difficult for beginners, but can help you to develop a strong ear as well as help you to develop your overall musicianship.

Basic Techniques

 How to hold the pick

First, curve the fingers of your picking hand inward, yet relaxed. Don't make a fist. Second, place the pick on top of the first knuckle, so that the point of the pick faces outward. Third, place your thumb over the pick to hold it in place. This may feel awkward or uncomfortable at first, but once you get used to it, you'll have full control over the pick.

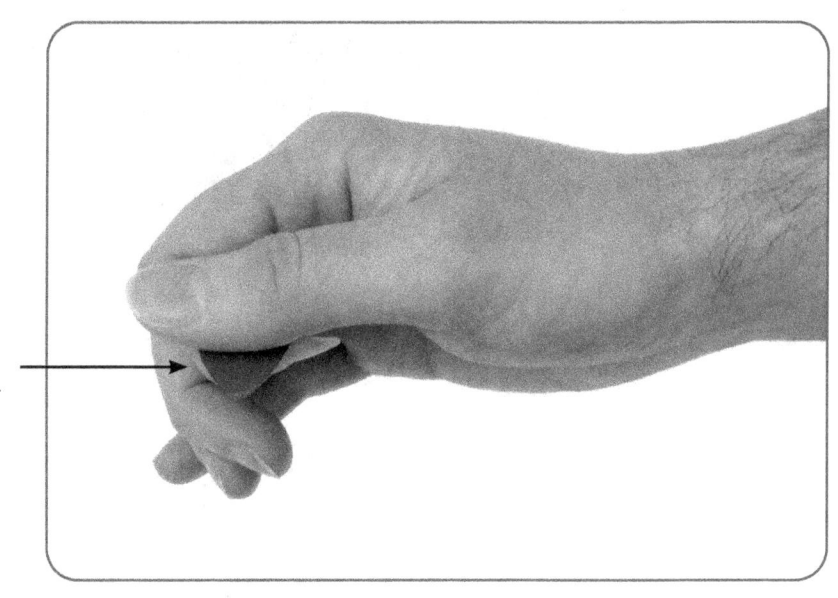

The pick lays on top of the knuckle of your index finger

 Not sure how to hold your guitar? We've included a video on this topic in the Beginner Guitar Essentials Course.

How to strum the guitar

When strumming, don't use your whole arm; simply swing from the wrist. To do this, start with your wrist slightly bent upward, then release the pick across the strings in a natural semi-circular motion. Don't force it or overthink it. Just let your picking hand glide over the strings.

The wrist angles up slightly

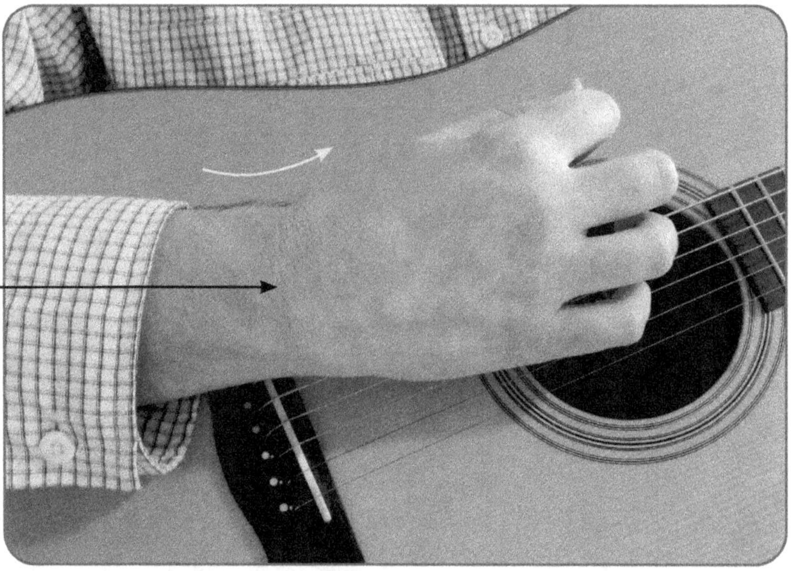

The arm stays in place, and the wrist moves

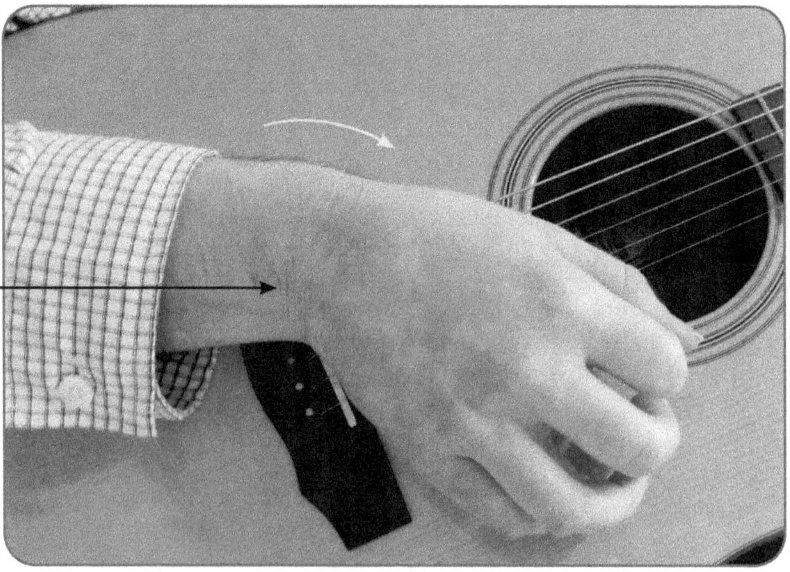

Tip:
It takes a while to develop control over this motion, but in time it will become second nature.

 Fret Hand Technique

Proper fret hand technique is crucial in order to get a good sound and avoid injury.

1. First, always keep your fingers up on their tips. The fingers should be spread apart and not touch each other.

2. Second, when playing a single note, do not press against the fret itself, but rather press just behind the fret on the fretboard. Pressing too far behind the fret will result in buzzing, so you'll want to make sure you are consistently pressing down just behind the fret.

3. Third, the wrist should be dropped down and the thumb planted behind the neck so that the thumb lines up between the index and middle fingers when looking at it from above.

4. Fourth, the knuckles of your hand should be running completely parallel to the neck, and the palm of your hand should not make contact with the neck.

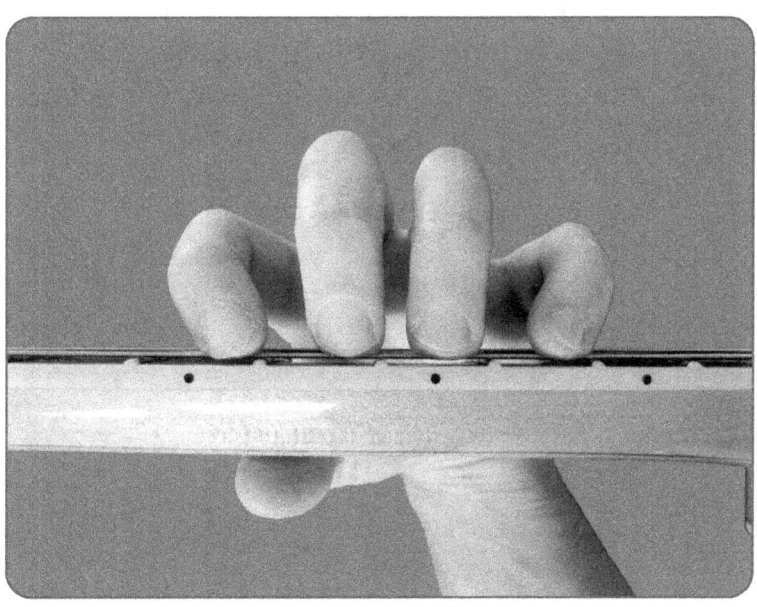

Best Practices for Practicing

Having a good practice plan and sticking to it is the best way to see improvement in your playing. In order to do this well, you'll need to put a plan in place that will help you figure out what you need to practice and when. The best thing to do, especially when you first start learning guitar, is to practice every day, even if it's just for a few minutes. This will keep your newly acquired knowledge fresh and constantly processing in the back of your mind, which helps you to learn faster.

1. Make sure you plan out what you are going to practice before you begin. This will give you a guide to work through as you go.

2. Consistency is key. If possible, practice at the same time every day. If that isn't possible, then at least figure out when each day you plan on practicing. Also, try to practice for about the same amount of time each session. When you first begin, fifteen to twenty minutes is usually a good amount of time. The more you learn and the longer you play, the more practice time you'll need.

3. Be sure to warm-up. Warm-ups can be any scale, finger exercise, licks, or riffs that help you focus on your technique so that you develop good habits while you practice. If you aren't sure what to play for a warm-up, check out *Technique Master Vol 1: 53 Warm-ups to Revolutionize Your Playing*.

4. Set your main goal for the day. It doesn't have to be a huge goal, just something you want to be able to do by the time you've finished. It can be as small as playing one note perfectly to as big as being able to play through twenty songs without a mistake. (Though you will need a couple of hours for that one).

5. Set aside time to review. You can review stuff you've been working on, older songs, or just about anything you wish.

6. Have fun and explore. Always take some time to discover new things about your instrument. Mess around, write songs, licks, make up chords. It doesn't always have to be good; it just has to be fun and get

you thinking about guitar in a new way.

7. Plan ahead. Once you are finished for the day, write down what you want to work on in your next practice session. That way the next time you sit down to play, you will be ready to go.

Tip:

For more on practicing, check out **Perfect Practice: How to Zero in on Your Goals and Become a Better Guitar Player Faster**.

How to Take Care of Your Guitar

Tips for caring for your guitar:

1. Change the strings every one to six months, depending on how often you play. The more you play, the more often you'll want to change your strings.

2. Always use the same gauge (size) strings, unless you want to adjust your neck and try and something new.

3. About once a year, be sure to clean and oil your fretboard. You can get fretboard oil at just about any music store.

4. Keep your guitar clean. However, do not use anything that can scratch the finish. A soft cloth or microfiber cloth should be used. To clean it, Windex will do, but there are also guitar cleaners and polishes you can buy that are specifically for the guitar.

5. Keep it out of the sun. The heat can melt glue and warp wood.

6. Keep it out of the cold. Cold weather shrinks the wood causing tuning and other intonation problems.

7. For acoustic guitars, consider getting a humidifier for your case. This will keep the wood from drying and cracking.

8. For electric guitars, be careful with the input jack. Even on expensive models these can become loose and fall off. They are easy to fix, but it's best to treat it well. Also, don't twist the cable when pulling it out of the guitar. This can cause the connections on the input jack to break off, and you'd have to solder the connections back together in order for it to work again.

9. When not playing it, keep your guitar away from vents and open windows. If possible, keep the guitar in its case in a place that maintains a constant temperature. Most guitars like it at about 76F degrees (24C).

10. For electric guitars, keep the pick-ups away from magnets and moisture.

Unit 2: Playing Chords
- Understanding Time
- Reading Neck Diagrams
- The Fastest Way to Learn Chords
- Common Chords
- Strumming
- Song Form

Time

The staff (shown below) is divided into sections called **bars** or **measures**. This is done to make the music easier to read.

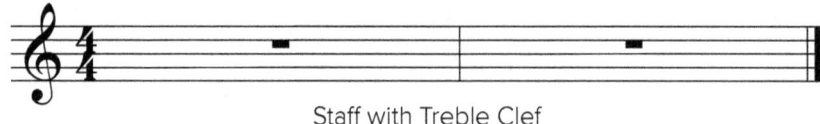

Staff with Treble Clef

Each measure is only allowed a certain number of beats. This limitation allows us to keep track of time. The grouping of these beats is called **meter**. The most common meter is four beats per measure called 4/4 time, as seen in the above example.

Beat is the underlying current of music. You don't necessarily hear the beat. Think of it as a second hand on a clock, a constant steady clicking that helps you keep track of time.

What you actually play is the **rhythm**. Rhythm tells you how long or how short a pitch or chord should be held. For example, in 4/4 time a whole note (see below) is sustained for four beats. A half note is sustained for two beats. A quarter note (which takes up a quarter of the measure) is sustained for only one beat.

Try it: Practice strumming the following rhythms

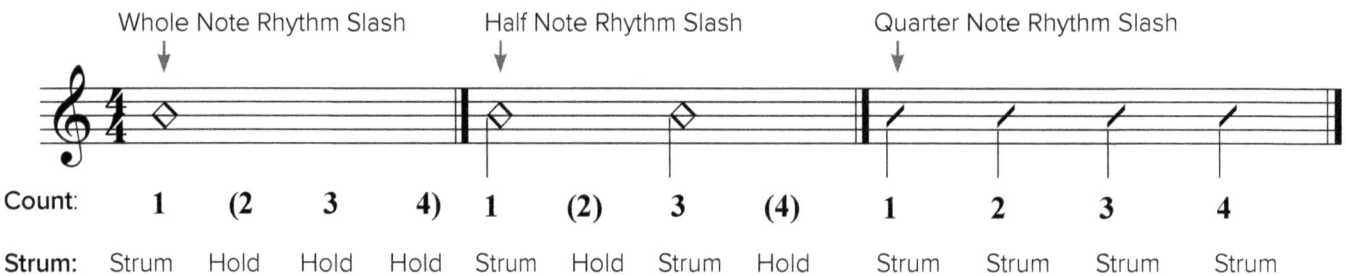

| Count: | 1 | (2 | 3 | 4) | 1 | (2) | 3 | (4) | 1 | 2 | 3 | 4 |
| Strum: | Strum | Hold | Hold | Hold | Strum | Hold | Strum | Hold | Strum | Strum | Strum | Strum |

Tip: You don't need to know how to read music to play the exercise above. The slash simply denotes the rhythm, not the note. You can practice this rhythm by strumming across the open strings (no chord).

How to Read a Fretboard Diagram

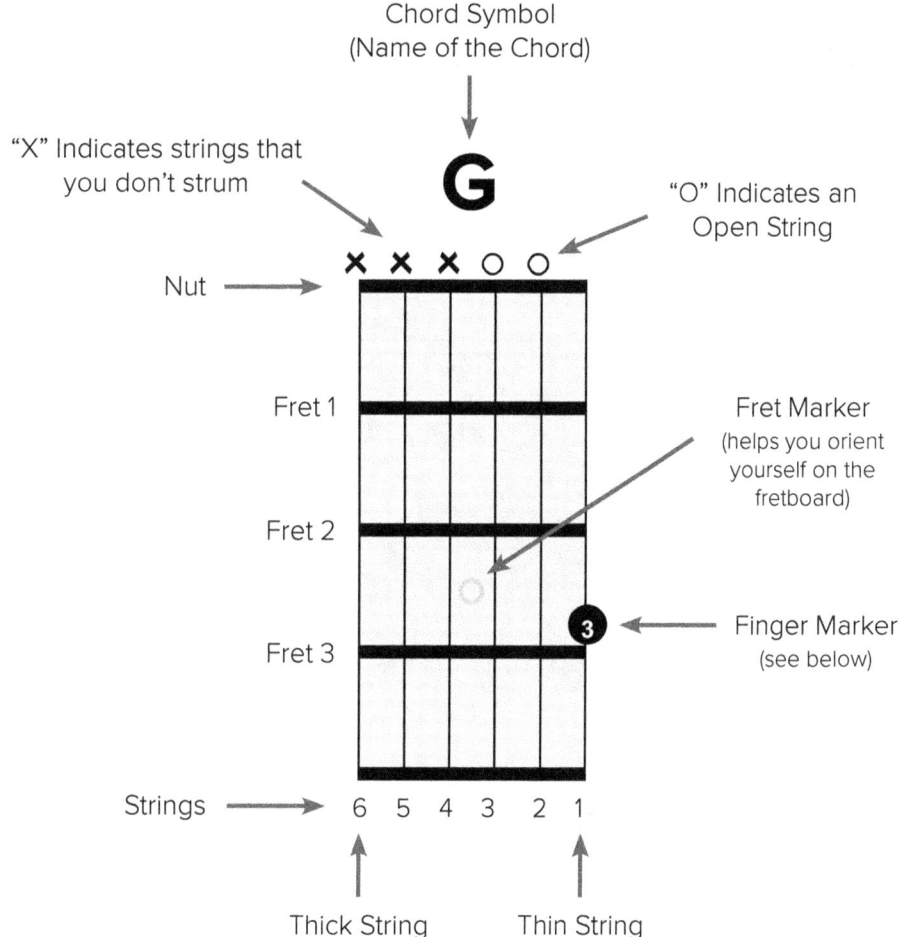

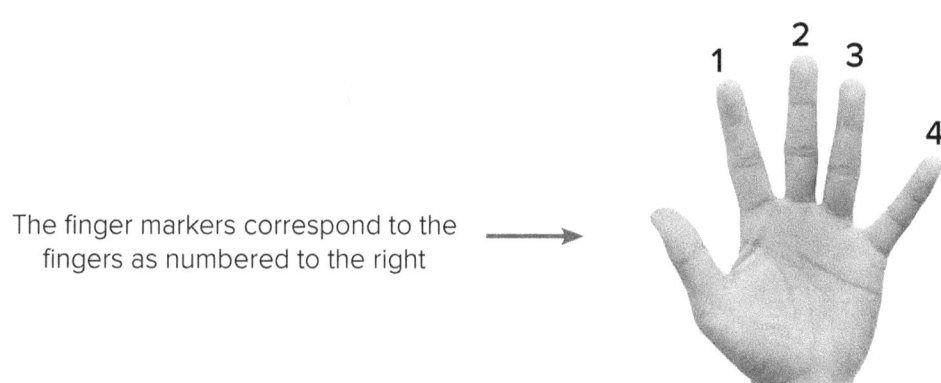

The finger markers correspond to the fingers as numbered to the right

---

Technique Tip:

When placing fingers on the fretboard, always keep your wrist dropped and your fingers on their tips. Remember only your fingertips and the thumb behind the neck should be touching the guitar. Keep the palm of your hand off the neck. This will help you build finger strength and solid technique.

Try it: Practice strumming using the G chord with the rhythms below.

Rhythm 1:

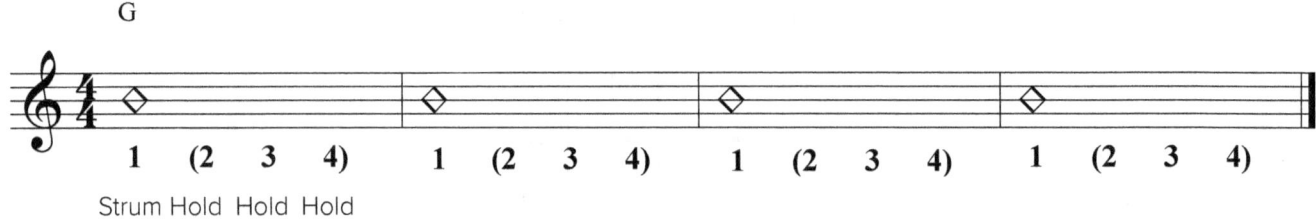

Rhythm 2:

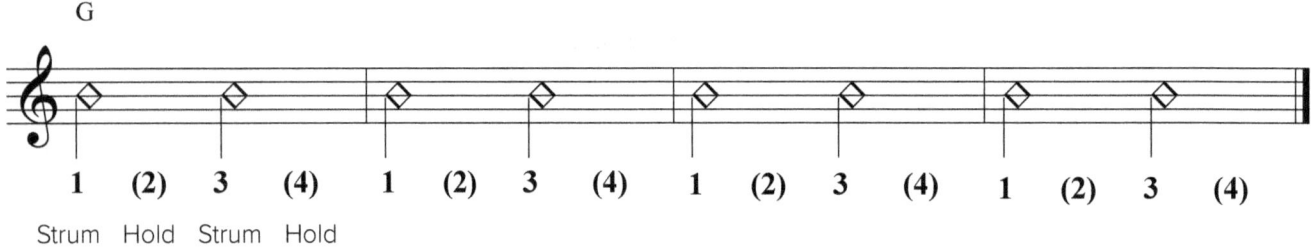

Rhythm 3:

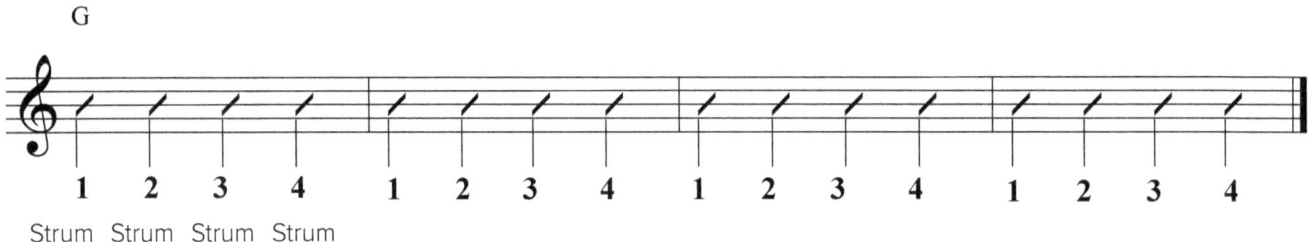

The Fastest Way to Learn Chords

Learning new chords can take time, so the best way I've found to speed up this process is through the use of **visualization**.

1. Place your fingers on the correct notes to form a chord, G for example.

2. Strum the chord to make sure you have it right.

3. Take a moment to memorize the placement of each finger individually. What fret and string is your first finger on, your second, your third, etc? Memorize what it looks like, what it feels like.

4. Once the finger placement is clear in your mind, take your fingers off the fretboard.

5. Look at your empty fretboard, and in your mind visualize where your fingers would be if you were playing the chord.

6. Now place your fingers back on the fretboard all at once. Don't place the fingers one at a time. Think of it as a shape, as a whole, rather than a series of finger placements.

Do this as often as necessary. Some chords will be easier to learn than others.

 Video Reference: Using Visualization to Learn Chords Faster

A Note About Changing Chords

Changing from chord to chord takes time and practice. So just be patient with yourself if you can't get the chords to change quickly enough right away. This happens to everybody who picks up a guitar. But if you stick with it, you'll eventually sound just like you want to.

 Video Reference: How to Change from Chord to Chord Smoothly

A Quick Lesson in Music Theory

Major, Minor, & Dominant Seven Chords

In music, any combination of pitches is considered a **chord**, so there are as many chords as there are combinations of sounds. Despite this seemingly endless number of possible combinations, most of them boil down to three primary types: major, minor, and dominant seven.

These labels refer to the sound the chord makes. So you could say a **major chord** sounds major, a **minor chord** sounds minor, etc. When comparing the sounds of these chords, minor sounds lower and darker than major, and **dominant seven** sounds like a more unstable version of major. These three sounds are the basis for a countless number of songs.

Chord Symbols

Throughout the unit, you will be learning major, minor, and dominant seven chords. When a chord is major, it will be shown by a single letter name (Ex: G). When a chord is minor, there will be a lowercase "m" next to the letter (Ex: Gm). The dominant seven chords will have the number 7 next to them (Ex: G7). These combinations of letters and numbers are called chord symbols.

 Video Reference: How to Read a Chord Chart

Easy Chords to Get You Started

Tip:
Notice the "X"s in each of the chord diagrams above. These mean that you don't strum those strings. The "O"s mean you strum the open string (no fingers on frets).

Rhythm 1:

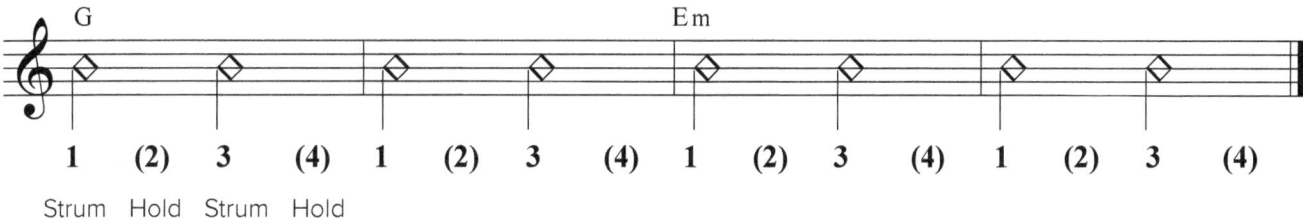

1   (2)   3   (4)   1   (2)   3   (4)   1   (2)   3   (4)   1   (2)   3   (4)

Strum Hold Strum Hold

Rhythm 2:

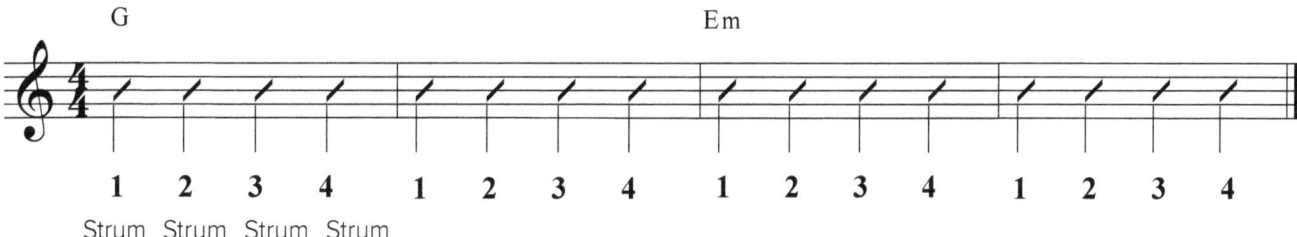

1 2 3 4   1 2 3 4   1 2 3 4   1 2 3 4

Strum Strum Strum Strum

29

 # G Major and E Minor

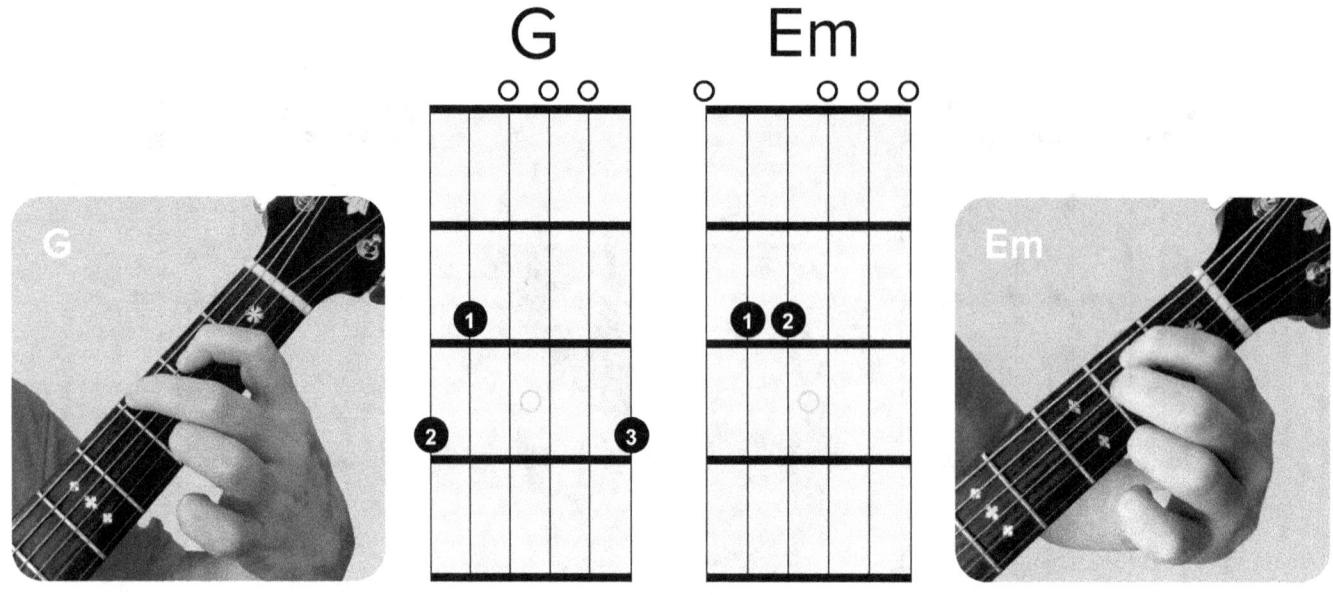

Try it: Practice the full versions of the G major and E minor chords using the rhythms below.

Rhythm 1: Video Reference: How to Change from Chord to Chord Smoothly

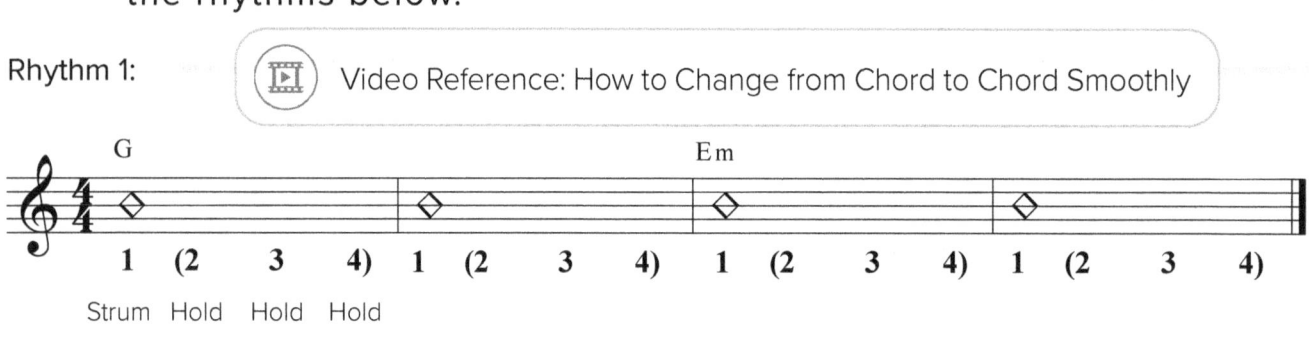

Rhythm 2:

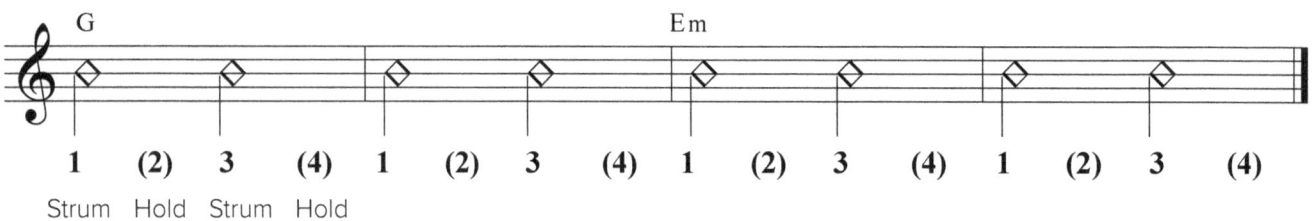

Rhythm 3:

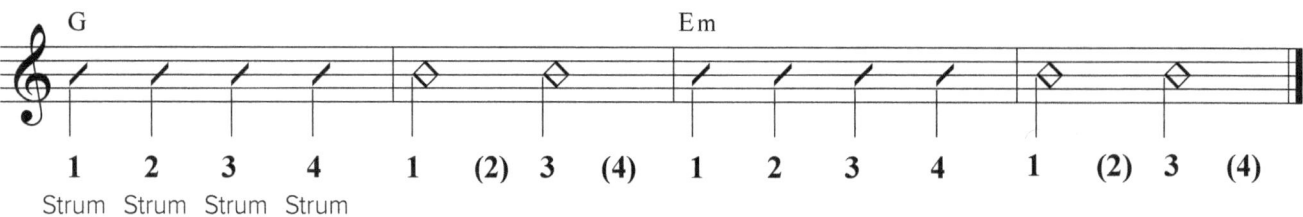

30

Practicing G and Em

Exercise 1: Strum the E minor chord. Do not pause or stop between measures, keep strumming clearly and evenly.

Exercise 2: Strum the G major and E minor chords.
Note: changing from chord to chord takes time at first, so be patient.

> **Tip:** When changing from G to Em, keep your first finger in place, then move your second finger from the last string to the fourth string. This will make changing between these chords easier.

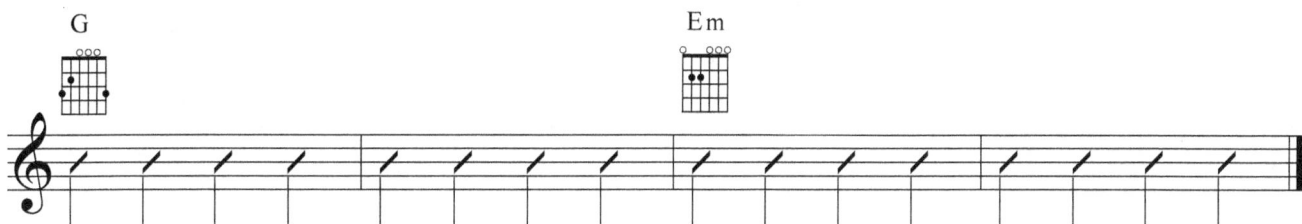

Exercise 3: Strum each chord four times evenly. Don't rush; make sure each strum is the same length as the last.

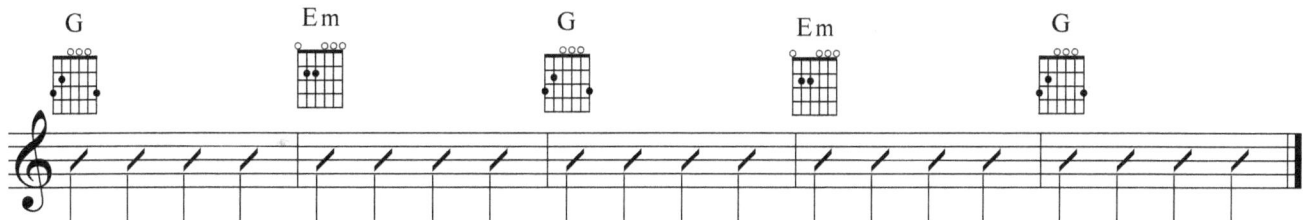

Exercise 4: In measures one and three, strum each chord twice.

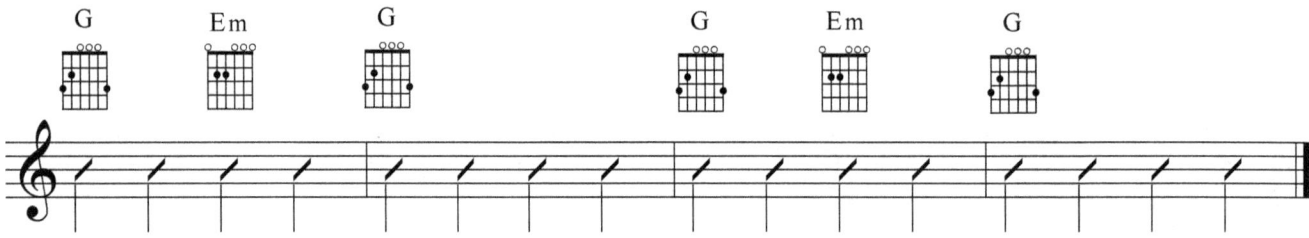

Exercise 5: Strum the Em and G chords. Be sure to go on to line two. The song doesn't end until the double bar line.

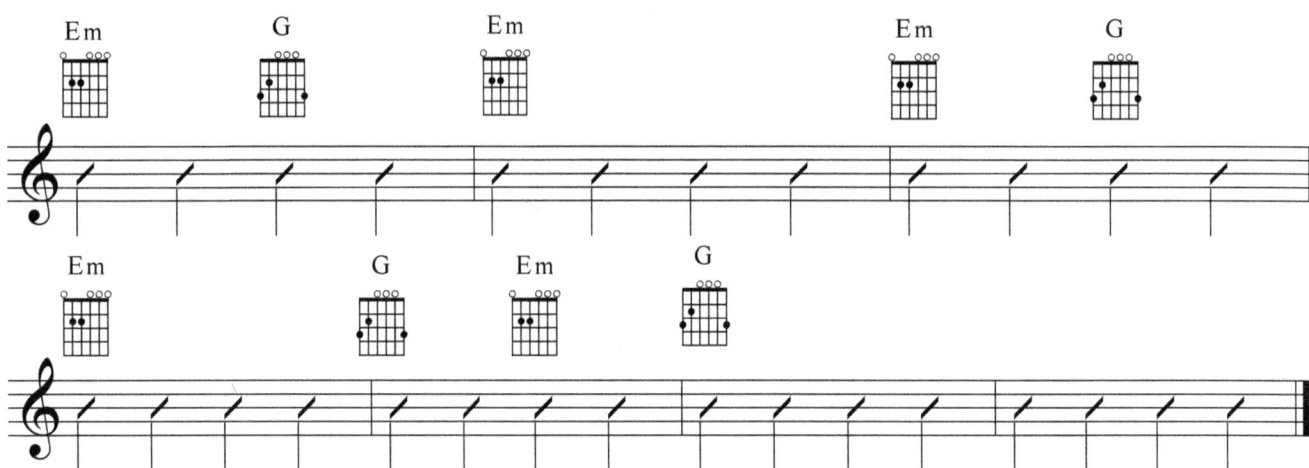

Be sure to review these exercises at least once a day, and make sure you take the time to memorize each chord before moving on to the next set.

D7 Chord

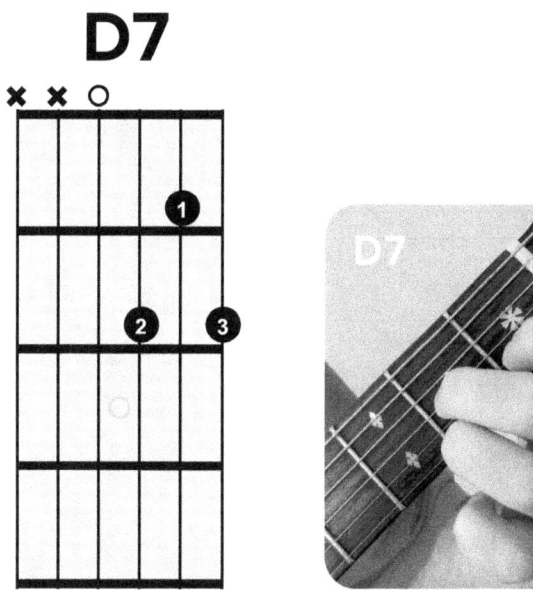

Try it: Practice the D7 chord below using the three different rhythms shown.

Note: Only strum strings 1-4 on this chord. The last two strings (the thickest strings) are not part of the chord (as indicated by the "X"s above the strings on the chord diagram above).

Tip:
Go slowly at first. Give your mind time to process everything. Also, be sure to fully memorize the chord shape and fingering.

Rhythm 1:

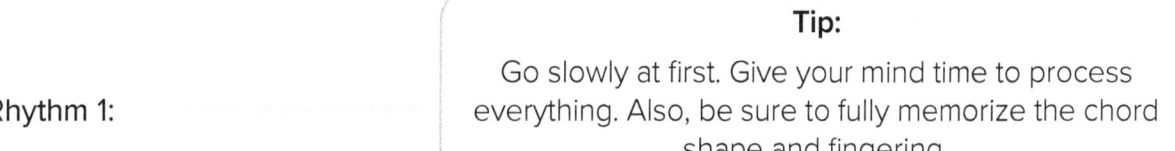

Rhythm 2:

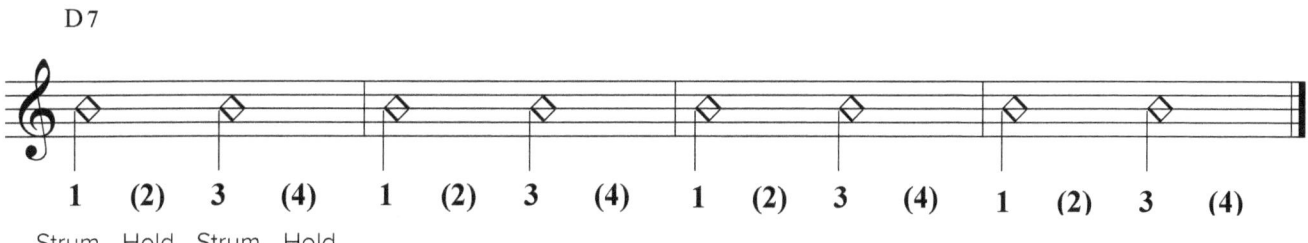

33

Rhythm 3:

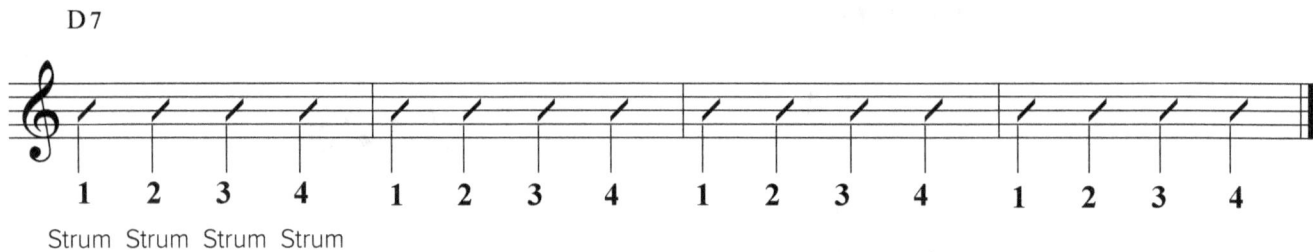

Strum Strum Strum Strum

Practicing D7

Exercise 1: Strum the D7 chord followed by the G chord.

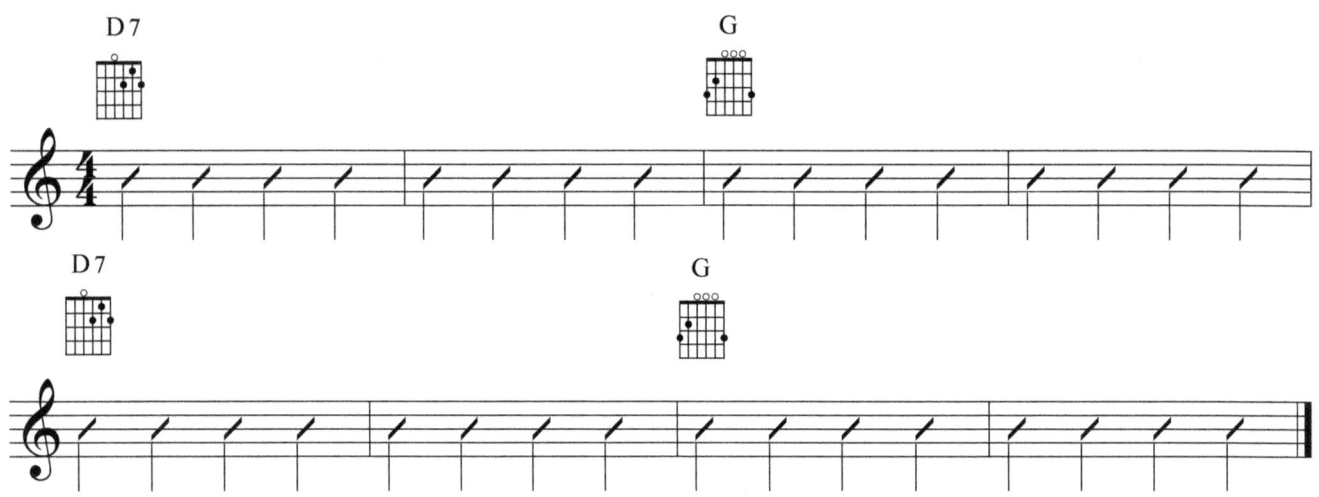

Exercise 2: Strum each chord four times evenly.

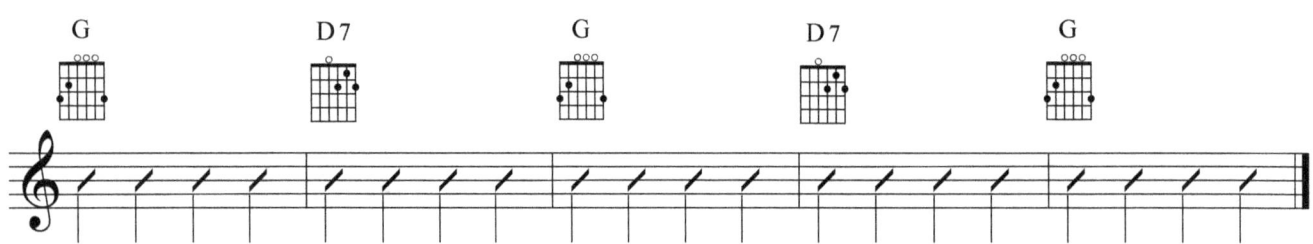

Exercise 3: Strum the following two line exercise.

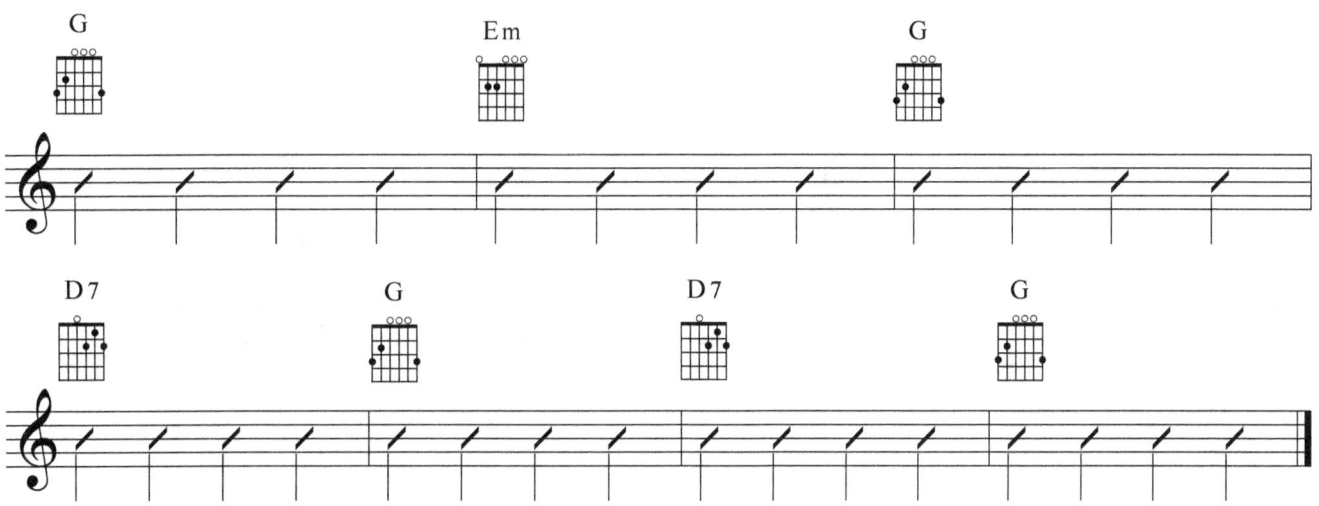

Exercise 4: Strum the following chords.

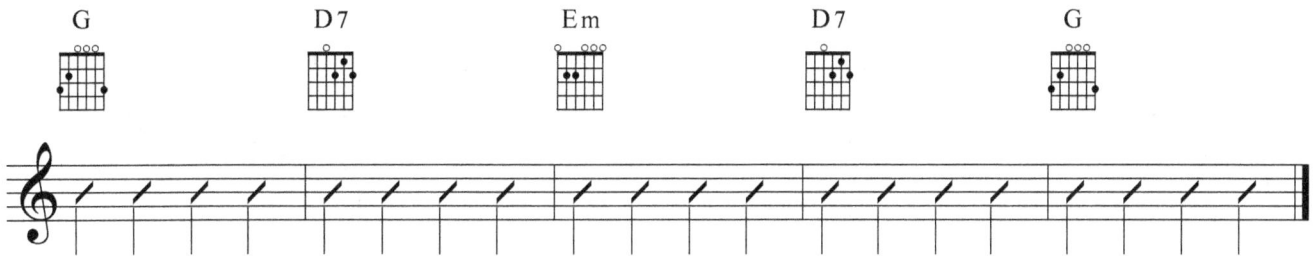

C Major & A Minor

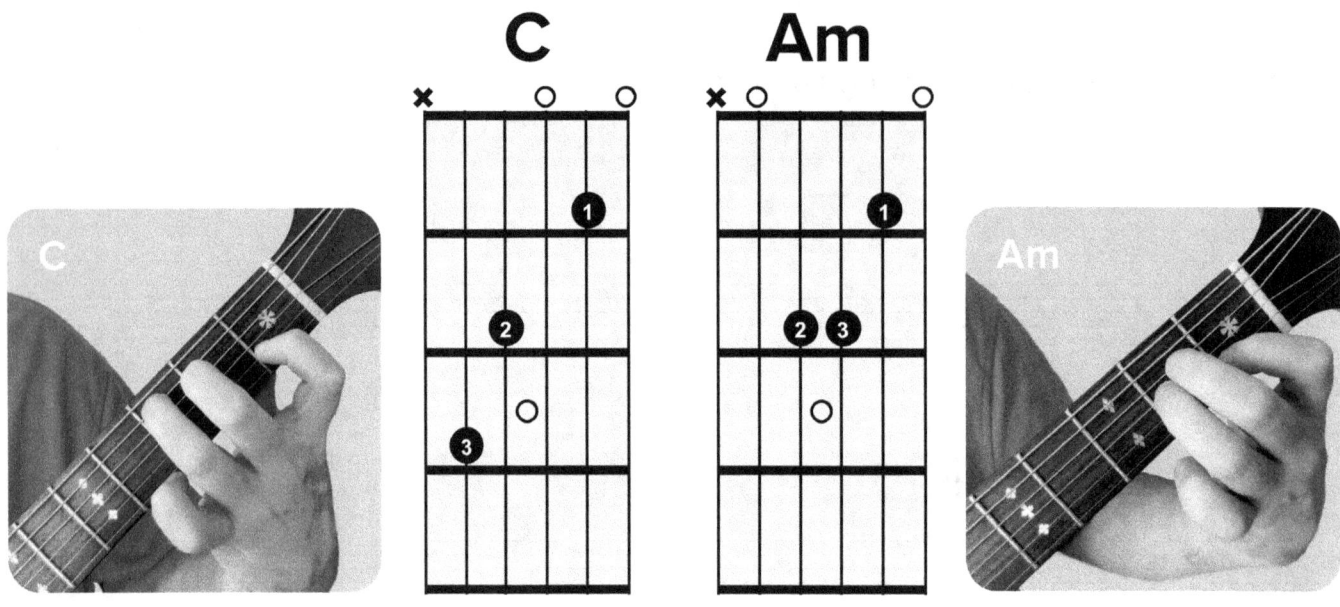

Try it: Practice the C chord below using the indicated strum patterns.

Note that for both of these chords you don't strum the last string (the thick string).

Tip:
Try the full C chord first. If needed, an easier version of the "C" chord uses only the first finger on the second string. This alternate version may be used, if needed, while you build finger strength.

Rhythm 1:

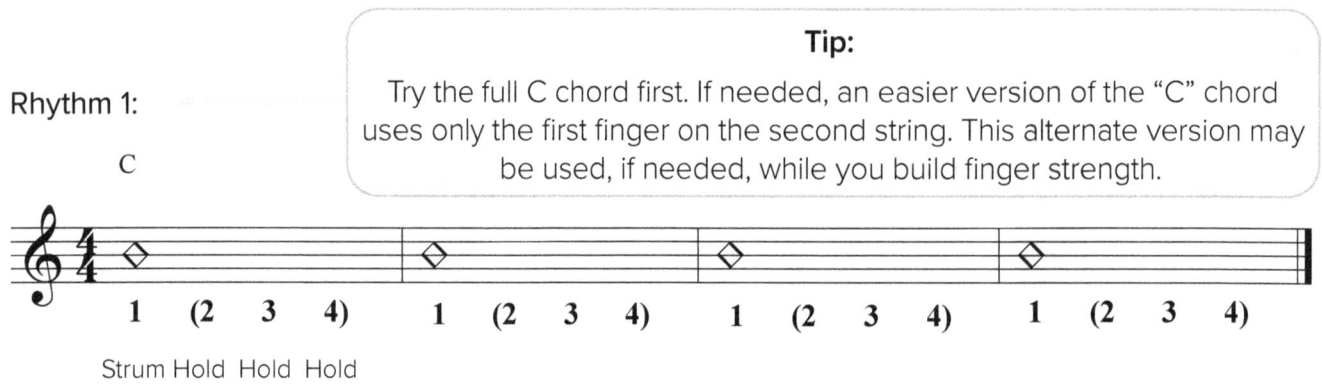

Rhythm 2:

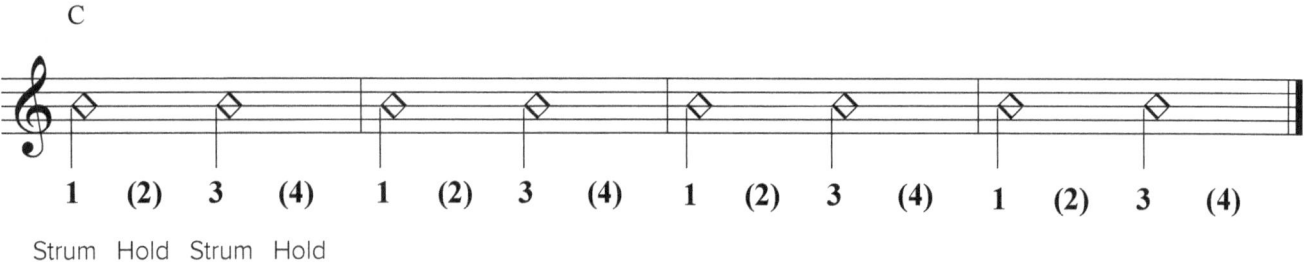

Rhythm 3:

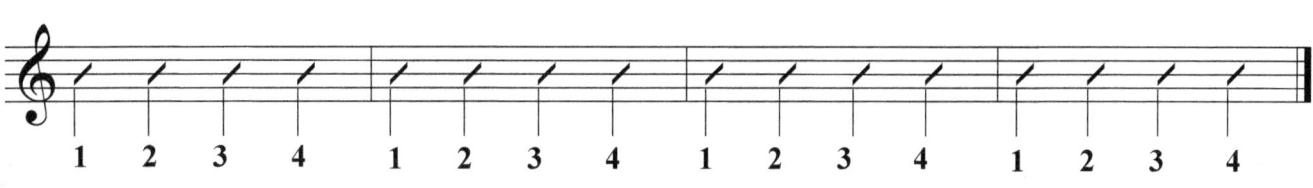

Practicing C and Am

Exercise 1: Strum the A minor chord.

Exercise 2: Strum the C and Am chords.

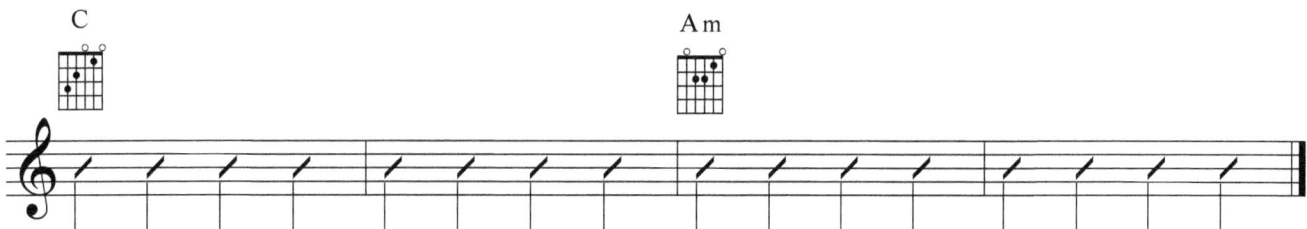

Exercise 3: Strum each chord four times.

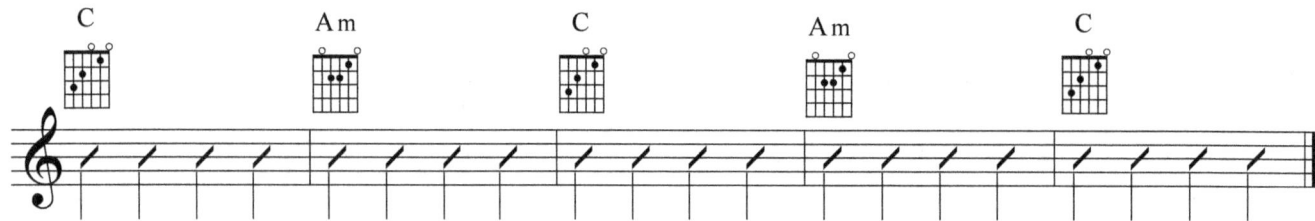

Exercise 4: In measures one and three strum each chord only two times.

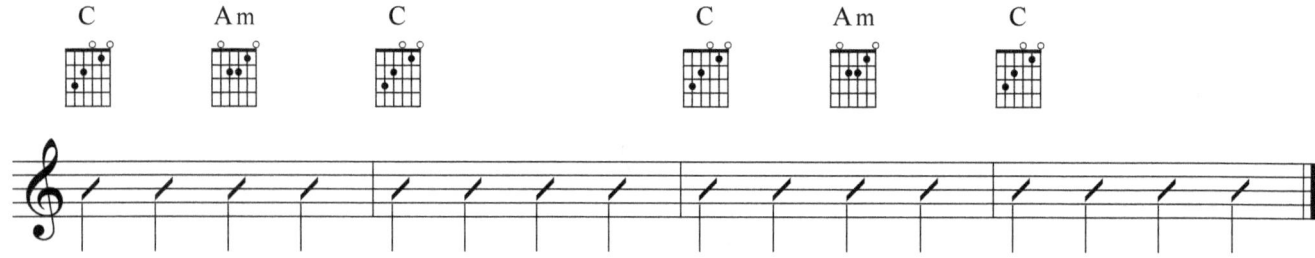

Exercise 5: Strum the C and Am chords in this two line song.

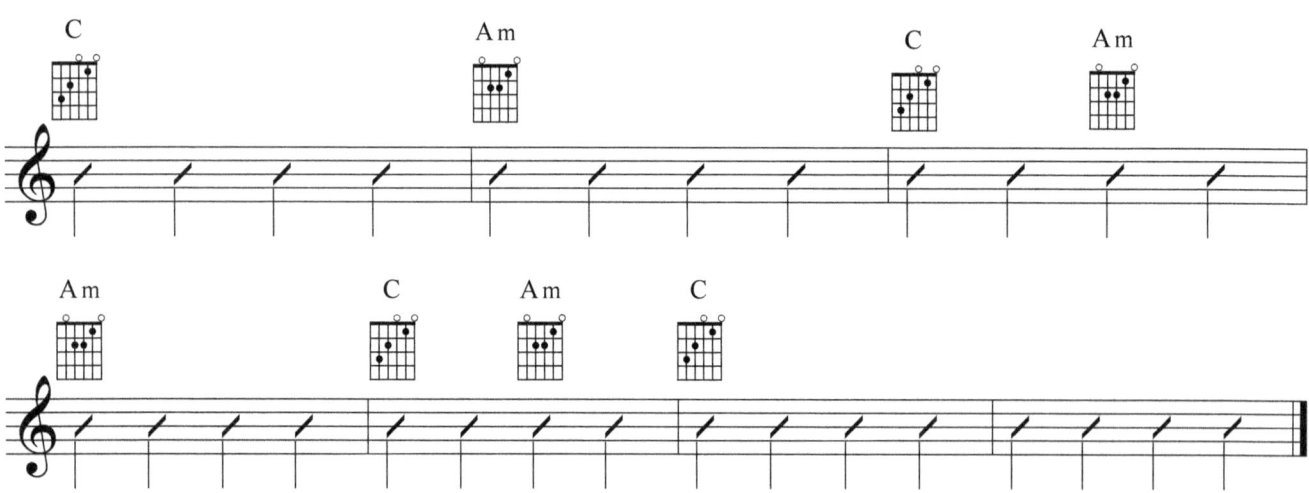

Review: G, Em, D7, C & Am
Using Common Chord Progressions

A **chord progression** refers to a series of chords and the sequence in which they are played. The next several chord progressions are the basis of thousands of popular songs.

Chord Progression 1: Note the half note rhythms in each measure.

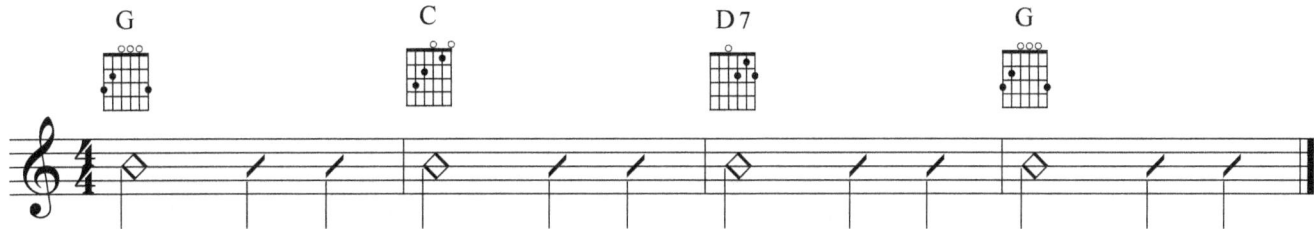

Chord Progression 2: Note the half notes in the final measure.

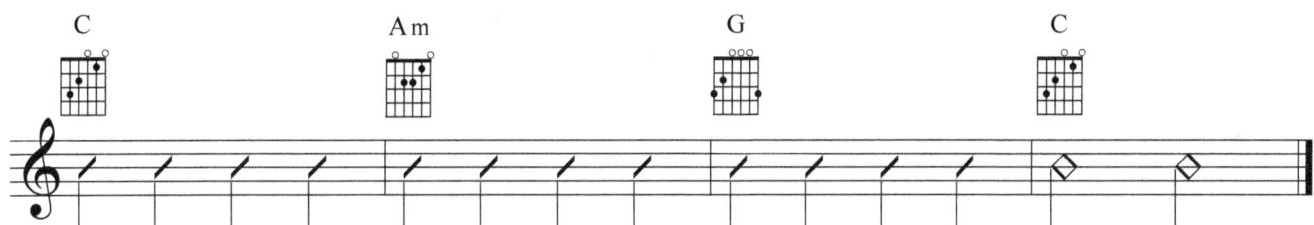

Chord Progression 3: The following progression is often called a turnaround chord progression and is the basis of countless songs.

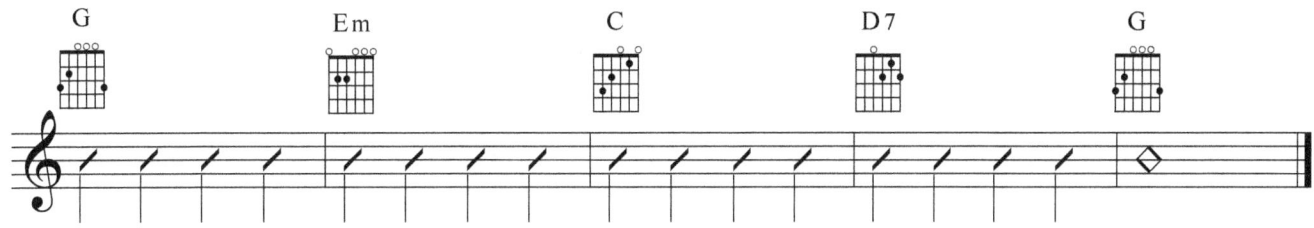

Chord Progression 4: Note the rhythm change in measure 3.

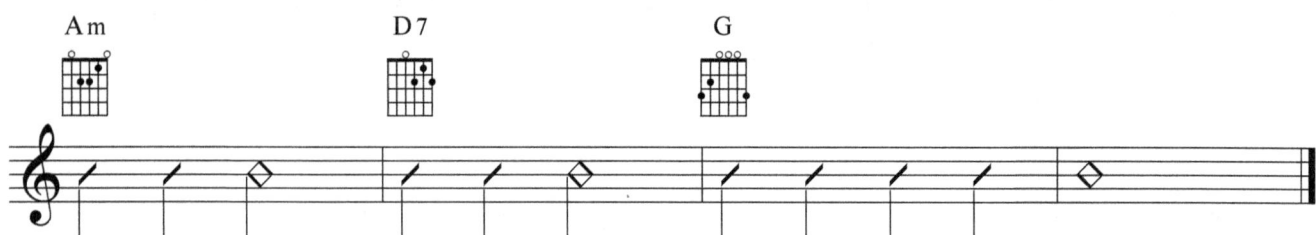

Chord Progression 5: This three line progression is called the **twelve bar blues**. As its name suggests, it originated with the blues. Today it has been adapted to just about every style of music.

Tip:
Even though it may seem easy to strum the G chord 16 times in the first line, it can be easy to lose track. Therefore, it is recommended that you count out loud as you strum.

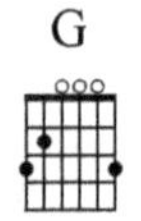

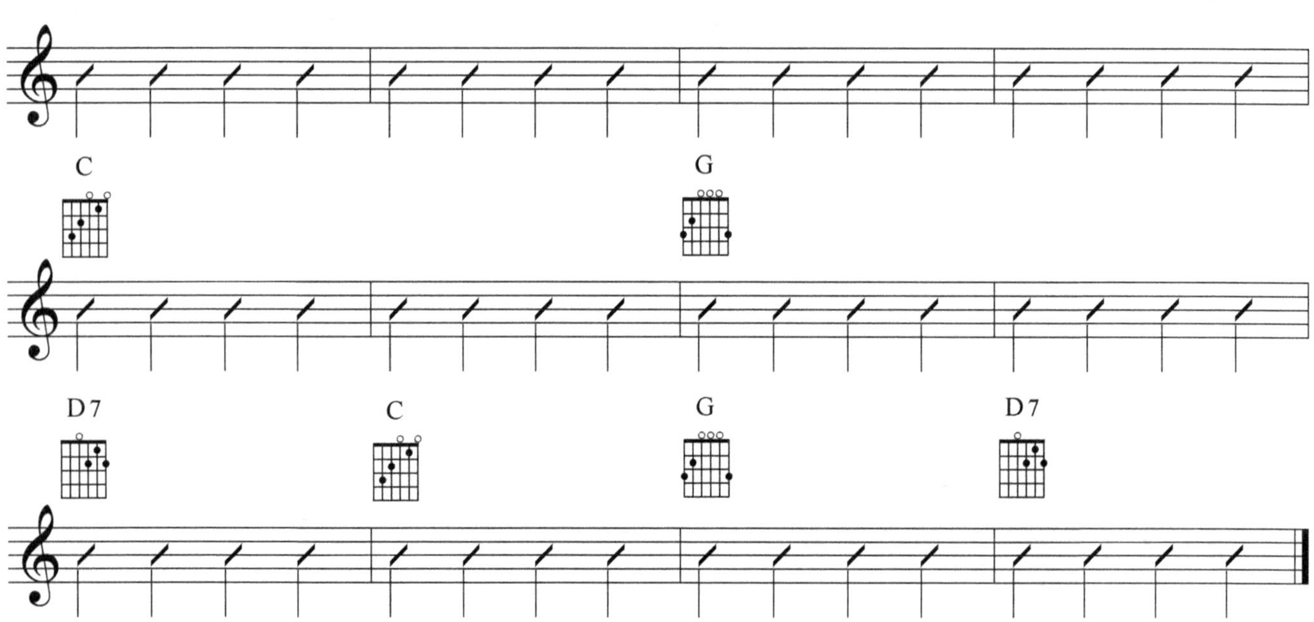

Song Form

On the next page, you'll get a chance to strum through a full song. Every song can be broken down into different sections. The first two most common sections are **verse** and **chorus**. This is done to help aid in memory, as well as to be able to refer to different parts of the song for rehearsal.

On top of that, a verse and a chorus will normally be different from each other, often times they will contrast in a variety of ways. The verse usually builds up to the chorus and then the chorus brings your ear back to the verse until the song comes to an end.

> **Tip:**
> The next song does not include chord diagrams. This is a common practice in many publications and websites, so it is always best to memorize the chord shapes.

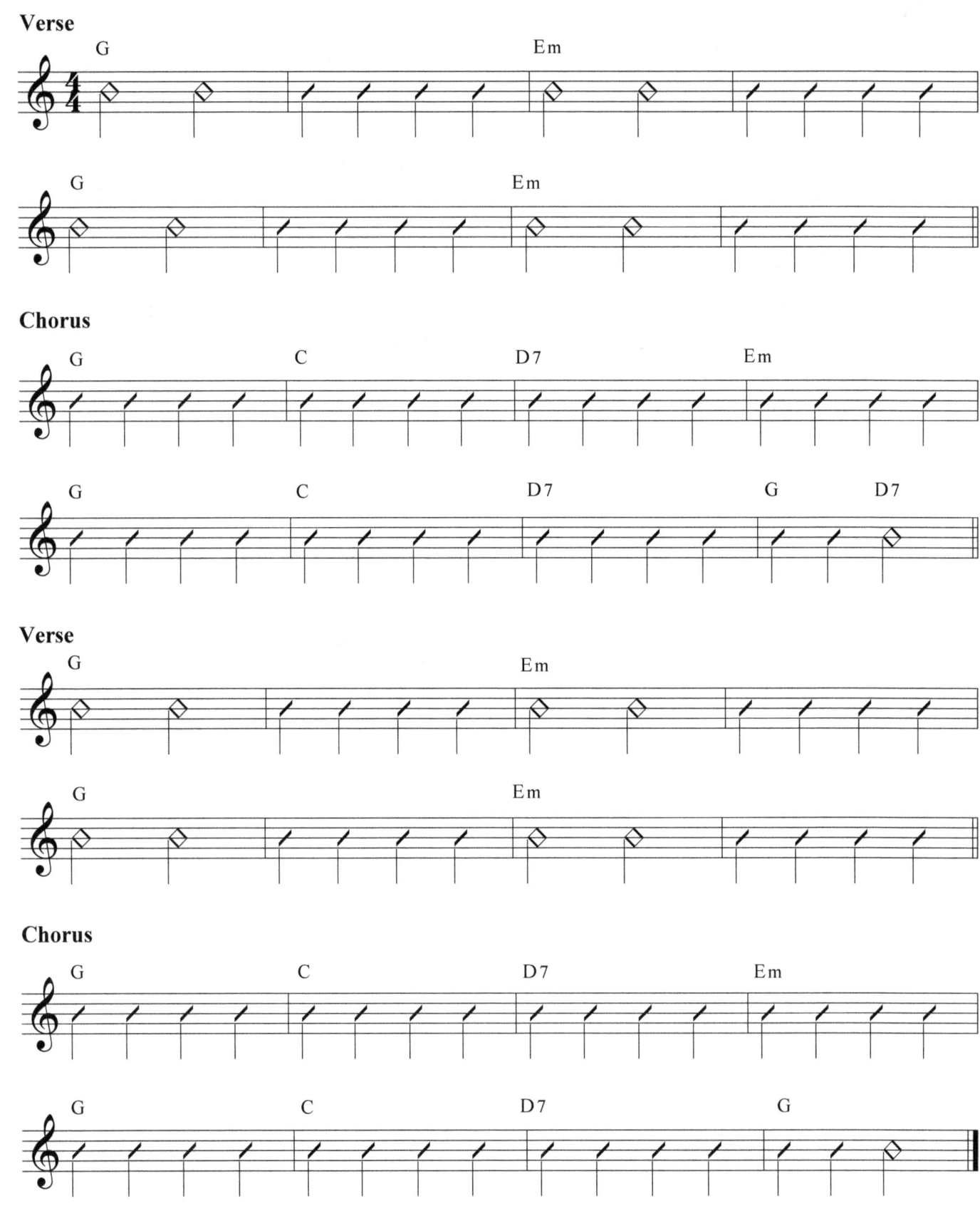

Eighth Note Strumming

⊓ = Strum Down
V = Strum Up

Step 1: Quarter Note Strum Review

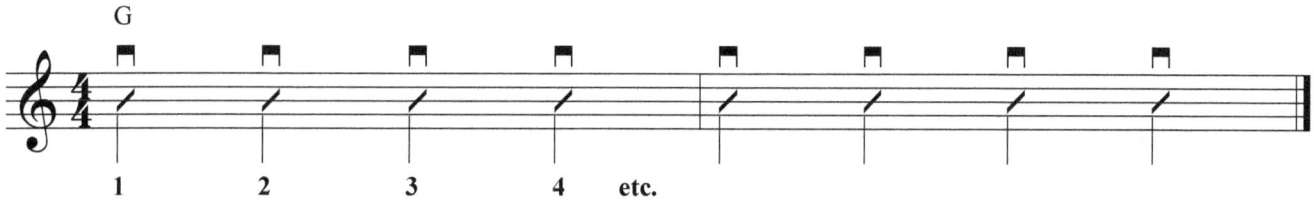

In the above example, each quarter note strum represents one full beat. We can divide each one of those beats in half. When this is done, the resulting notes are called eighth notes.

When strumming eighth notes, you strum the first half of the beat downward and the second half of each beat upward. (See Step 2).

Step 2: Eighth Note Strums

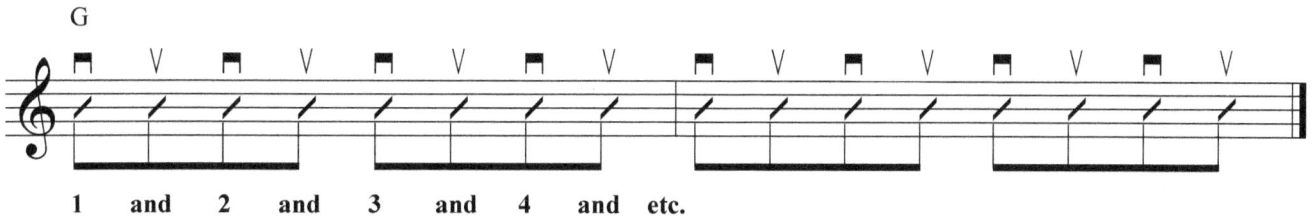

43

Step 3: Combining Quarter and Eighth Note Strumming

Exercise 1:

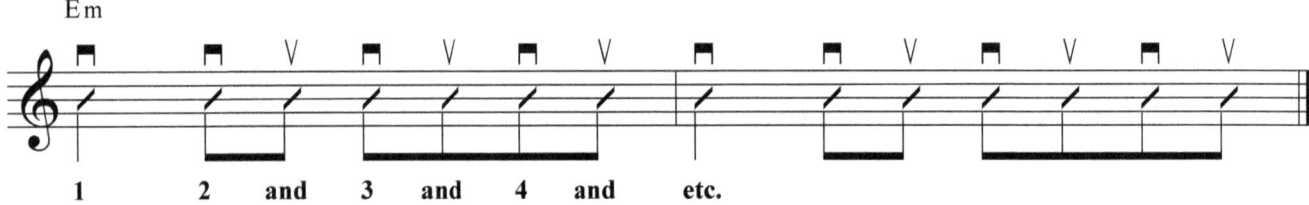

Exercise 2:

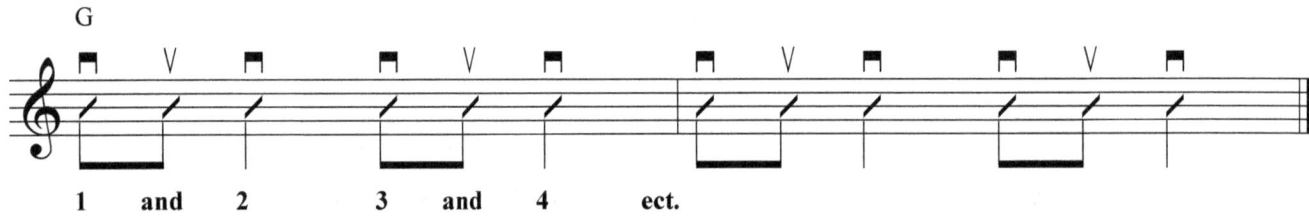

3/4 Time

In music, not everything is grouped in fours. Many times the beat will be grouped in groups of 3 instead. This is shown at the beginning of a song in the time signature.

- **Four-four time** means that you have four beats per measure and that the quarter note is the beat.

- In **three-four time**, you have three beats per measure and the quarter note is the beat here as well.

The easy way to remember it is this: in four-four count to four per measure, in three-four count to three.

Try it: Practice strumming the chords below in 3/4 time.

> **Tip:**
> Remember, for each measure, count to 3.

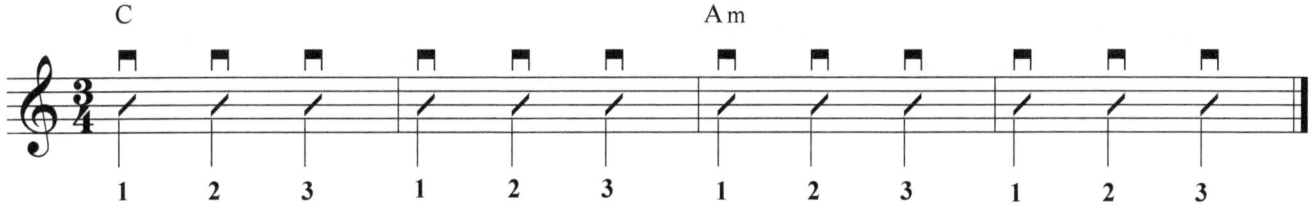

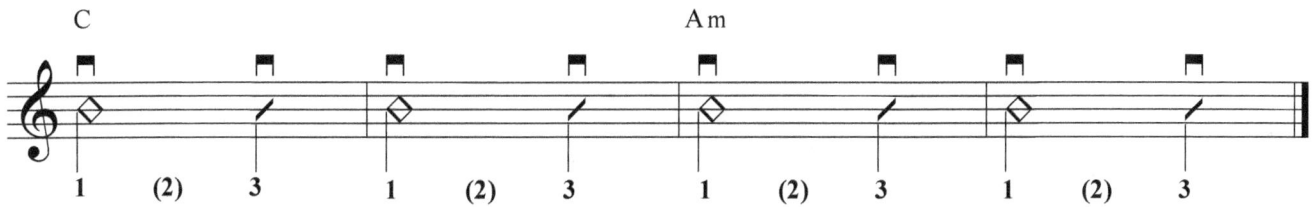

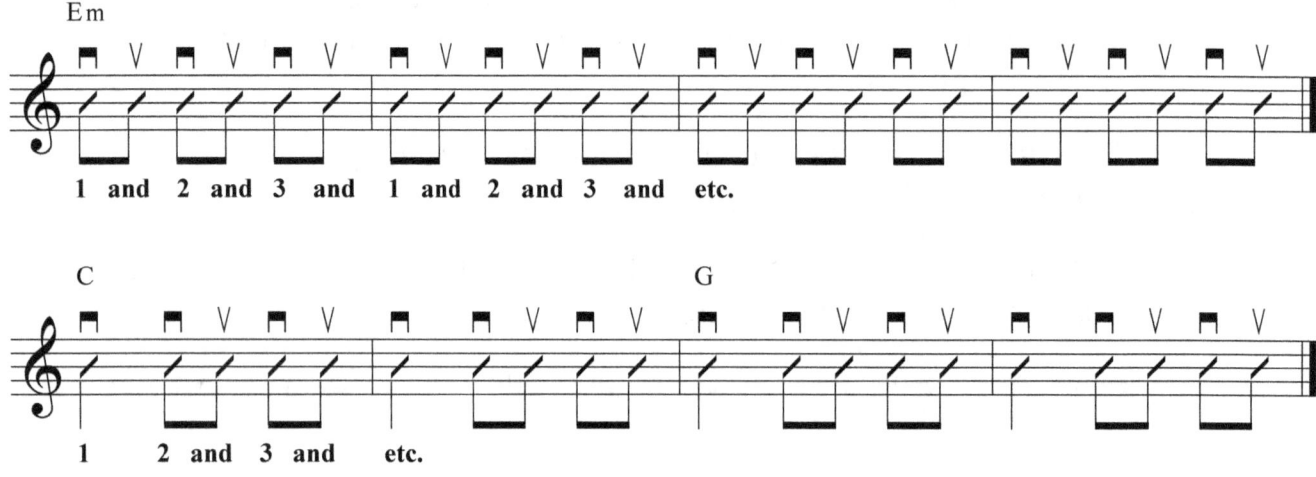

Dotted Half Notes

Since a **whole note** (worth four beats) cannot be used in three-four time, a dot is placed next to the half note, extending it to a full three beats. (See below). Note: this **dotted half note** can also be used in four-four time in the same manner.

Try it: Practice strumming the dotted half notes using the G chord.

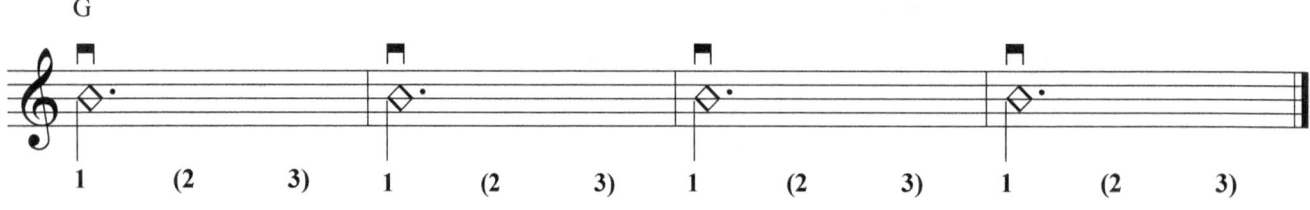

Practicing in 3/4 Time

Exercise 1:

Exercise 2:

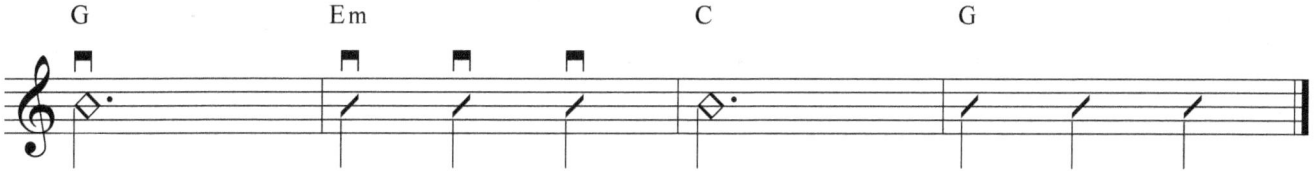

Exercise 3:

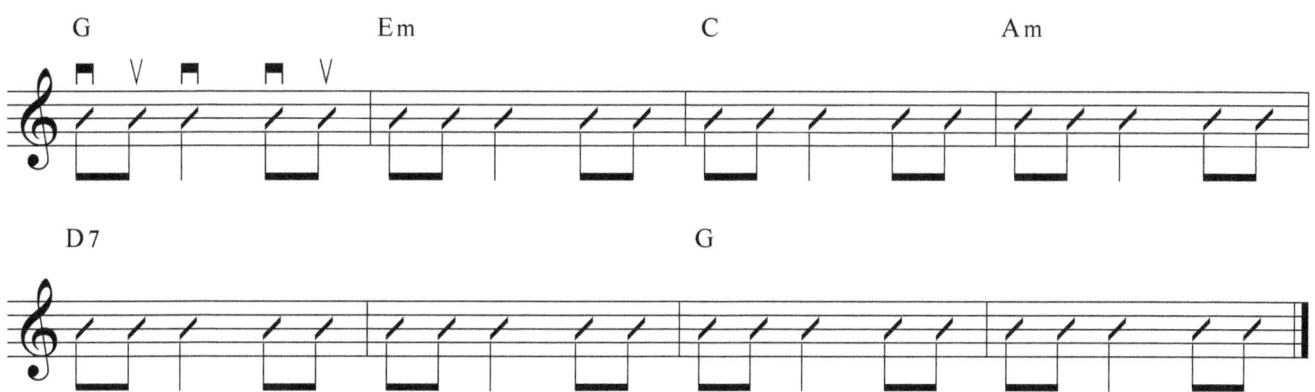

Exercise 4:

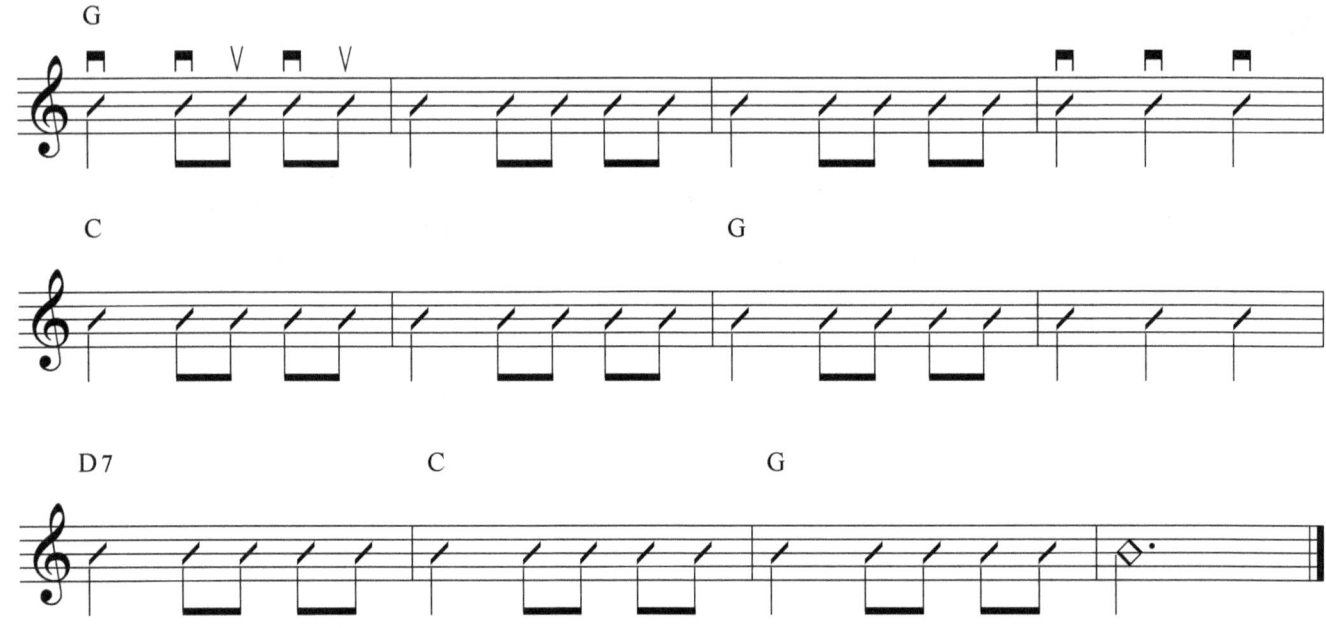

Rests

Rests are short moments of silence in music. They can give pieces of music much needed space, places to breath, so to speak. When playing them on guitar, a rest means that you have to stop the sound of the guitar for the duration of the rest. This can be accomplished by placing the picking hand over the strings to stop the sound. You can also, in some cases, use the fretting hand to stop the sound. Each rhythmic value has a corresponding rest. (See below.)

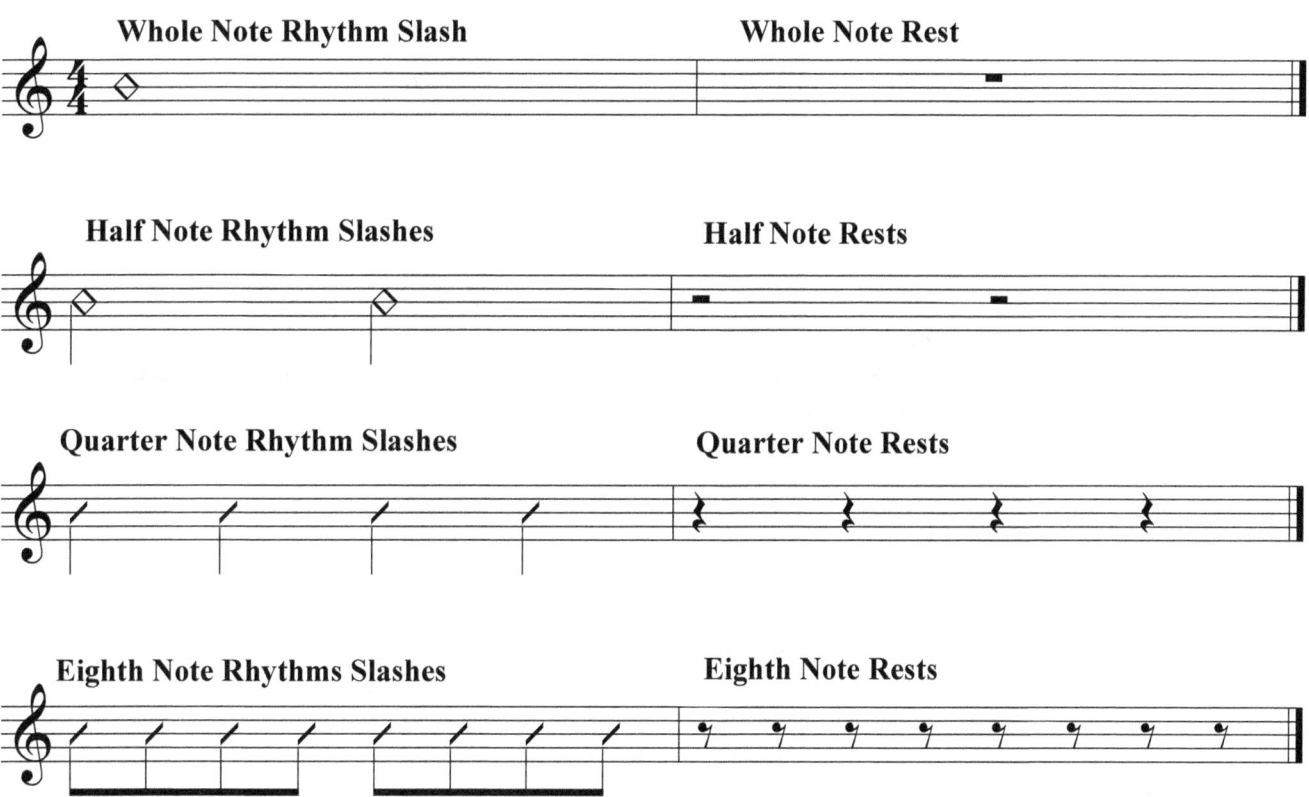

Ties

A **tie** is a curved line that connects two rhythms together in order to extend the length of the rhythm. So when you see a tie, you strum the first note but not the second one. (See below).

Try it: Practice playing ties using the rhythms below.

Rhythm 1:

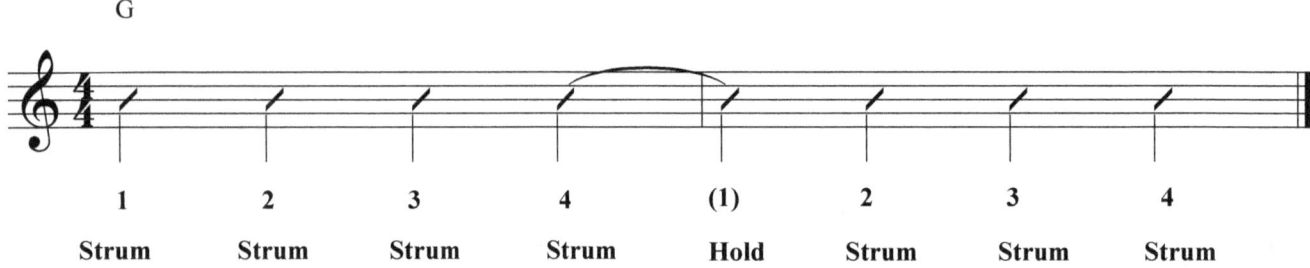

Rhythm 2:

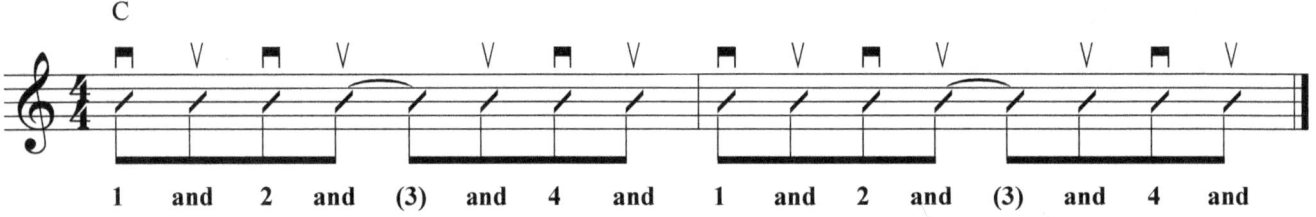

Rhythm 3:

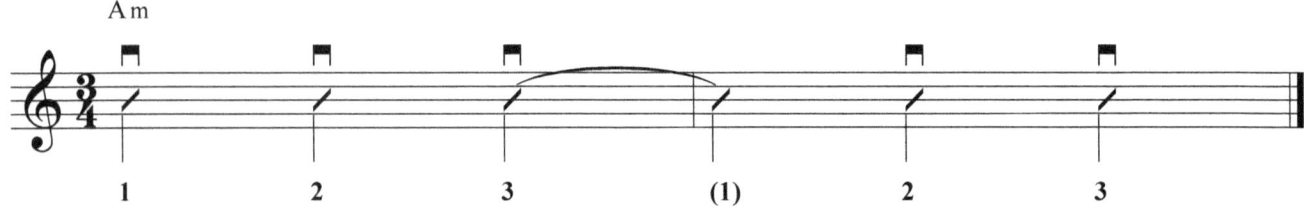

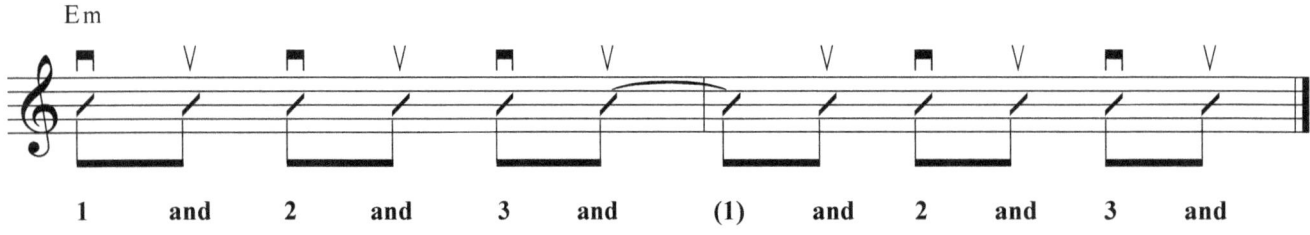

Practice Ties and Rests

Exercise 1:

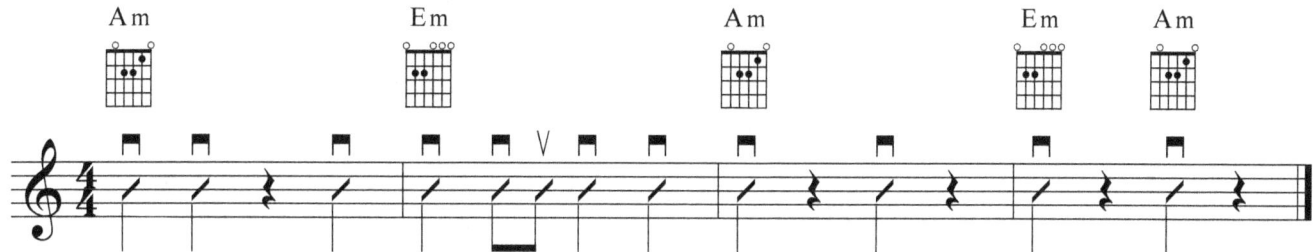

Exercise 2:

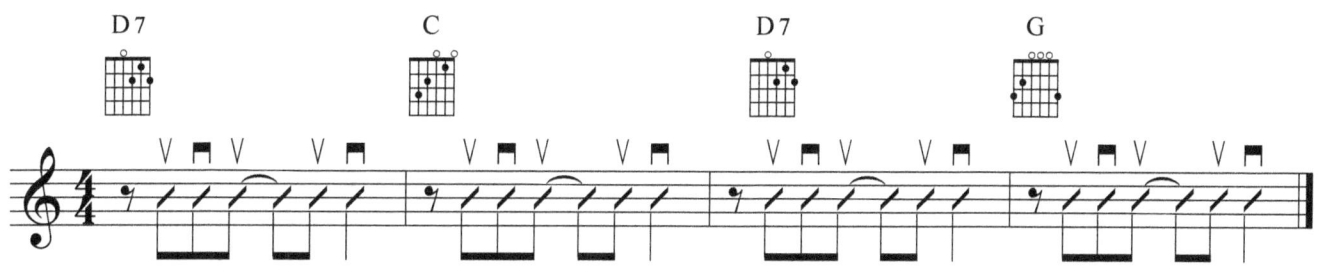

Exercise 3:

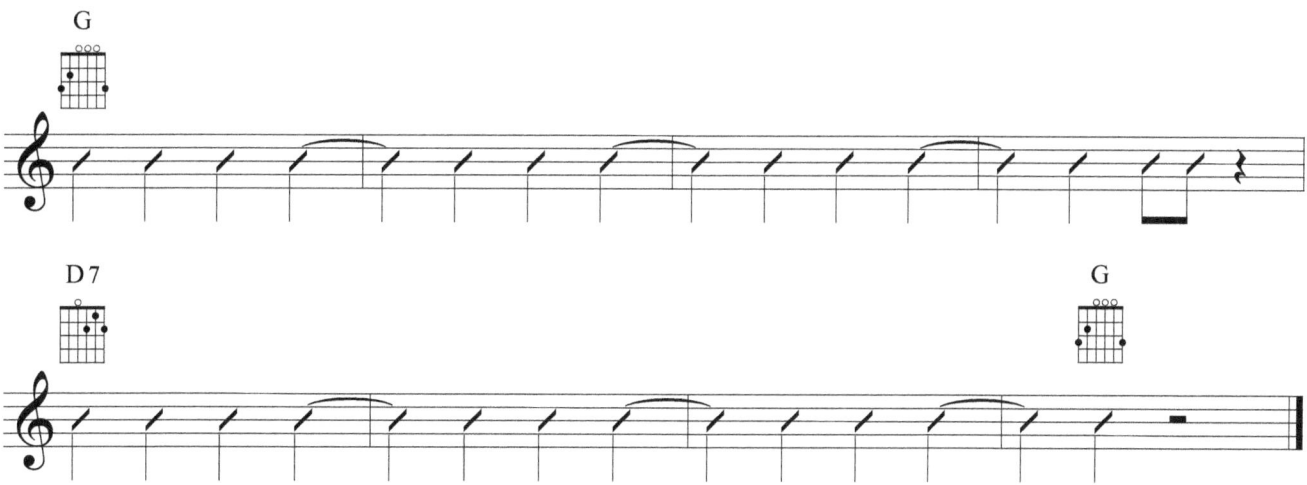

Tip:

The chords you've learned so far are just the beginning! We'll cover power chords in Unit 6, and there is a chart of common chords included in the Appendix. For those who would like to learn more, we created *Guitar Chord Master*. This series of books focuses exclusively on chords and strum patterns, and it covers open chords, power chords, barre chords, how to use a capo, moveable shapes, and much more. Find out more at TheMissingMethod.com.

Unit 3: Reading Music

- The Basics
- Understanding Time
- Note Reading in Open Position
- Accidentals

The Elements of Reading Music

The Staff

Long ago there was no universal system to keep track of what a song sounded like. For a very long time, the only way to have a record of a song or piece of music was to pass it on from musician to musician by ear. Eventually someone decided to place a circle on a line and call it a specific pitch. After some time, more lines were included and the modern staff was born. The staff is simply a chart showing the highness and lowness of pitches. The lower a dot (or notehead) is on the staff, the lower the sound and vice versa.

In order to know which range of pitches to perform, clefs were used. A clef is a symbol that tells what notes to expect on the staff. There are several clefs in music, but for guitar we only need to learn one: the treble clef. (Though it is recommended to learn bass clef as well in order to develop your overall musicianship.)

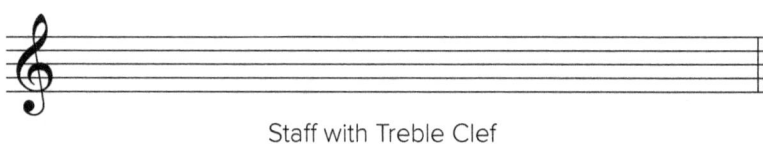

Staff with Treble Clef

The treble clef tells you what specific notes, or pitches, you can expect to find on its lines and spaces. The lines are (from low to high) E G B D F. The spaces are F A C E. Many elementary schools teach a pneumatic device to help you remember these note names: Every Good Boy Does Fine. And of course the spaces spell FACE.

Ledger Lines

It is possible to go higher and lower than what is on the staff. When this is done, the extra notes are placed on lines called ledger lines.

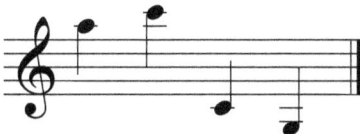

In music there are a total of 12 notes that can occur at different pitch levels. Each different sound is given a letter name. Thus the musical alphabet consists of A B C D E F G. However, this represents only seven of these notes, the remaining five notes fall in between these. These notes will be discussed later in this unit.

Time

Time works the same with notation as it does with chords (from the previous unit). However, instead of slash notation, traditional notation is used. See below.

Try it: Practice with whole notes, half notes, and quarter notes
  Note: Use any open string to try these out.

Exercise 1:

Exercise 2:

Exercise 3:

Eighth Notes

Just like with chord strums, a quarter note can be further broken down into two eighth notes, each representing half a beat. When performing eighth notes, pick down on the downbeat, and up on the second half of each eighth note pair.

Practice with eighth notes

Exercise 1:

Exercise 2:

 # Notes on the First String

Play the E note on the first string open. (Open means with no fingers).

Play the F note on the first string, first fret with the first finger.

Play the G note on the first string, third fret with the third finger.

Video Reference: Combining Pitch and Rhythm, Part 1

Whole Note Exercise

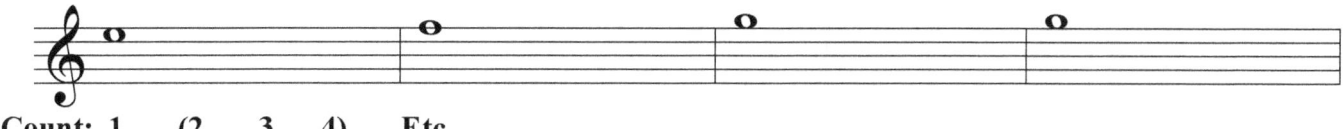

Count: 1   (2   3   4)   Etc.

Half Note Exercise

Count: 1   (2)   3   (4)

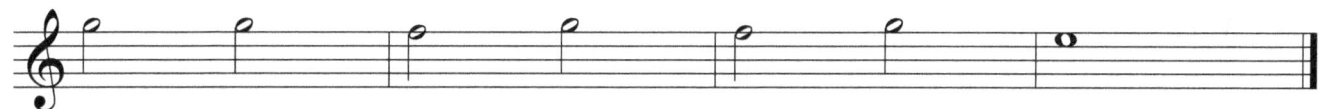

Quarter Note Exercise

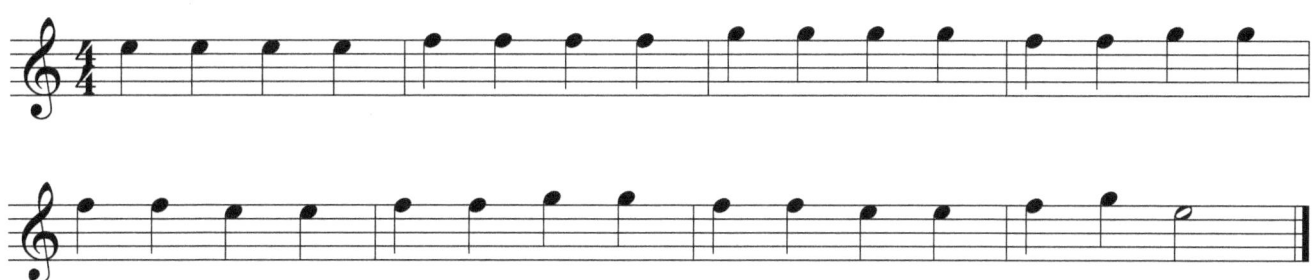

Eighth Note Exercise

> **Tip:** When playing eighth notes, be sure to alternate your picking. Pick down on the beat, and up on the off beats (the &s of the beat.)

Rain Drops

 # Notes on the Second String

Play the B note on the second string open.

Play the C note on the second string, first fret with the first finger.

Play the D note on the second string, third fret with the third finger.

Video Reference: Combining Pitch and Rhythm, Part 2

Second String Exercise

Eighth Note on the Second String

Three Notes Eight Measures

All Around

The following song contains notes from both the first and second strings.

Ode to Beethoven

 # Notes on the Third String

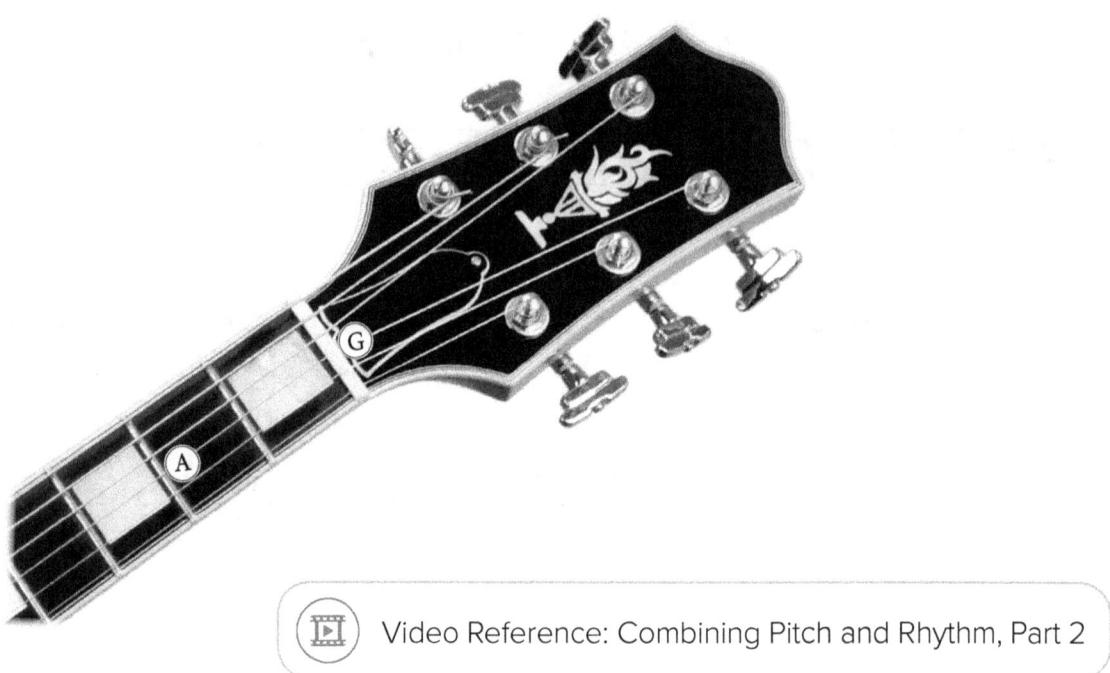

Video Reference: Combining Pitch and Rhythm, Part 2

Play the G note on the third string open.

Play the A note on the third string, second fret with the second finger.

Third String Exercise

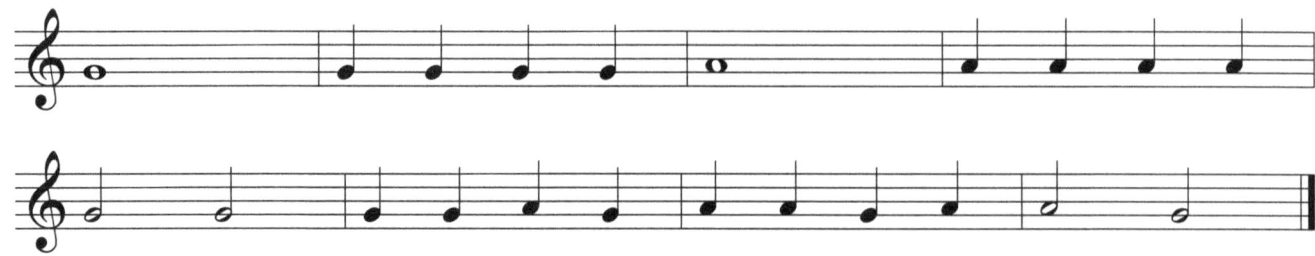

Third String Practice

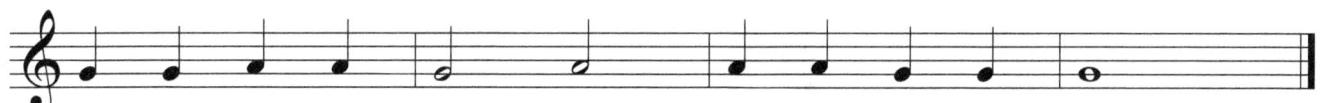

More G A Practice

The next three songs contain notes from both the second and third strings.

Story of the Sea

Waving to the Waves

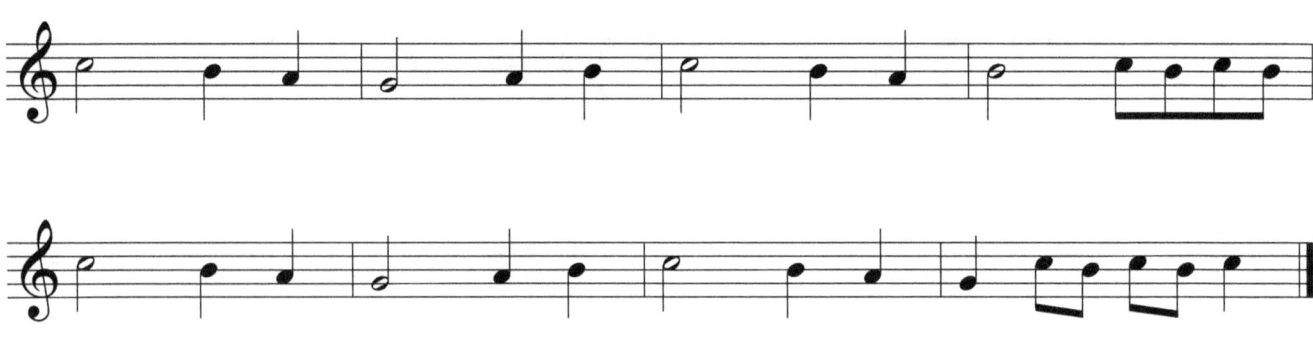

The Duke of Blues

Review the First Three Strings

The following songs use all three strings.

Piano Jump

Bass Fishing Blues

 # Notes on the Fourth String

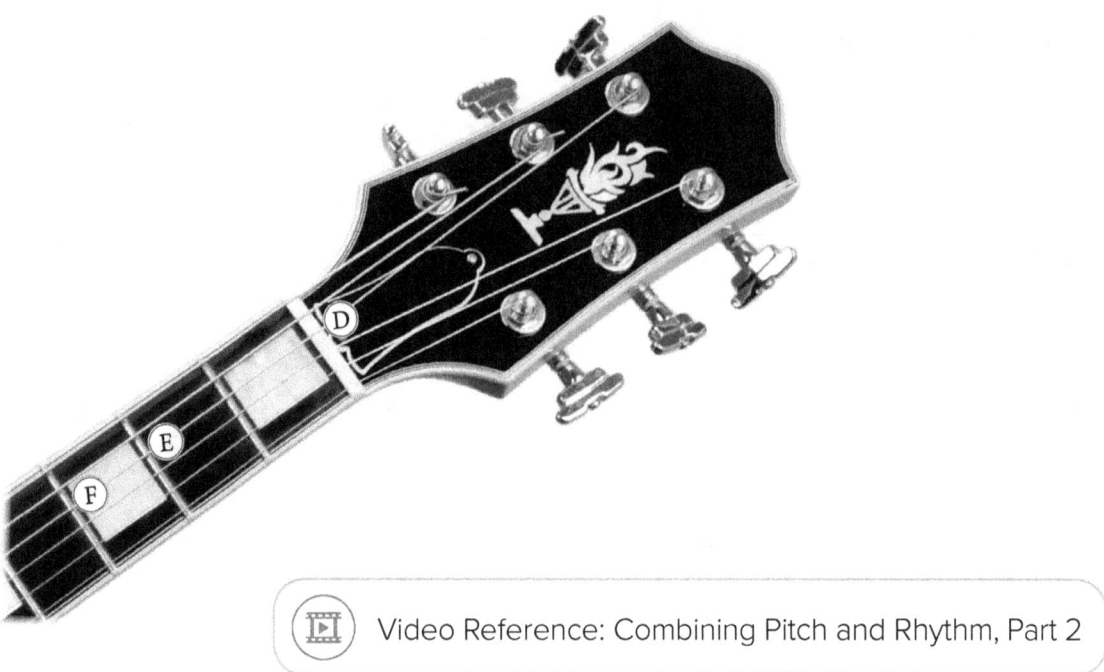

Video Reference: Combining Pitch and Rhythm, Part 2

Play the D note on the fourth string open.

Play the E note on the fourth string, second fret with the second finger.

Play the F note on the fourth string, third fret with the third finger.

Fourth String Practice

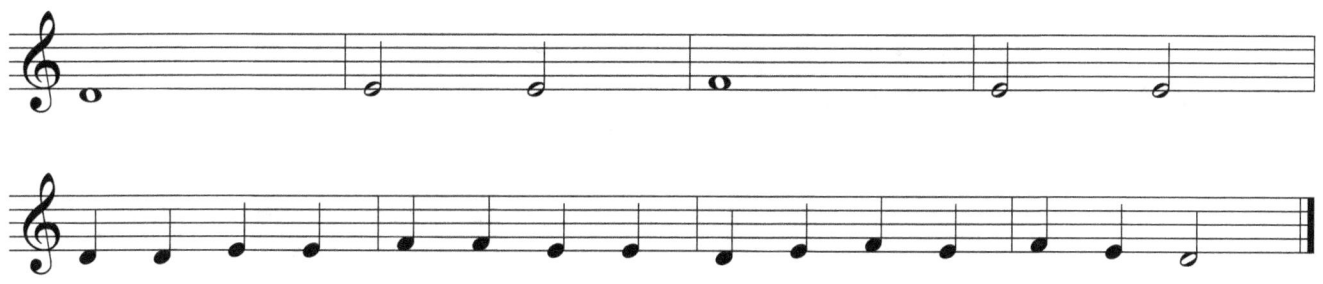

Practice D E F

The next songs will use a combination of both fourth and third strings.

Park Ranger

On the Run

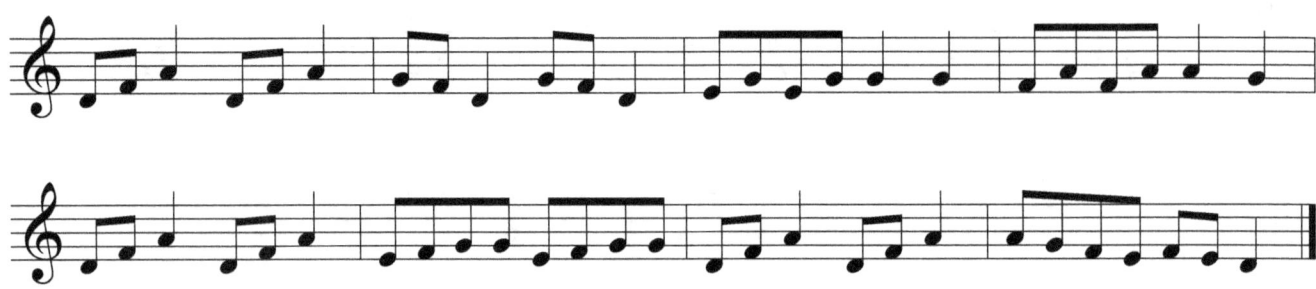

The Sinking Snowman

Review Strings 1 through 4

The next songs will utilize strings 1-4.

Late Again

Like a Diamond

 # Notes on the Fifth String

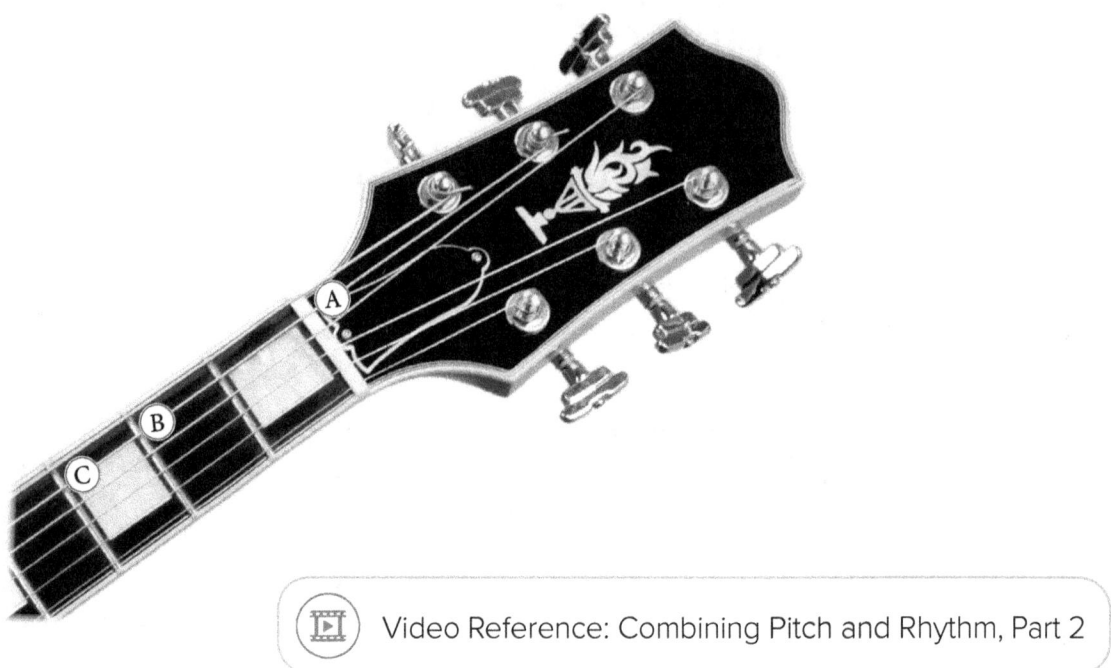

Video Reference: Combining Pitch and Rhythm, Part 2

Play the A note on the fifth string open.

Play the B note on the fifth string, second fret with the second finger.

Play the C note on the fifth string, third fret with the third finger.

Fifth String Practice

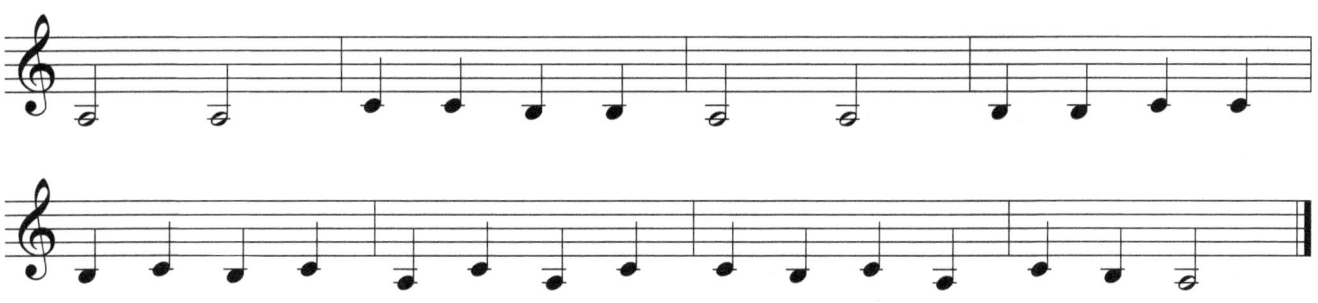

Fifth String Exercise

The following songs use only the fifth and fourth strings.

Don't Get Caught

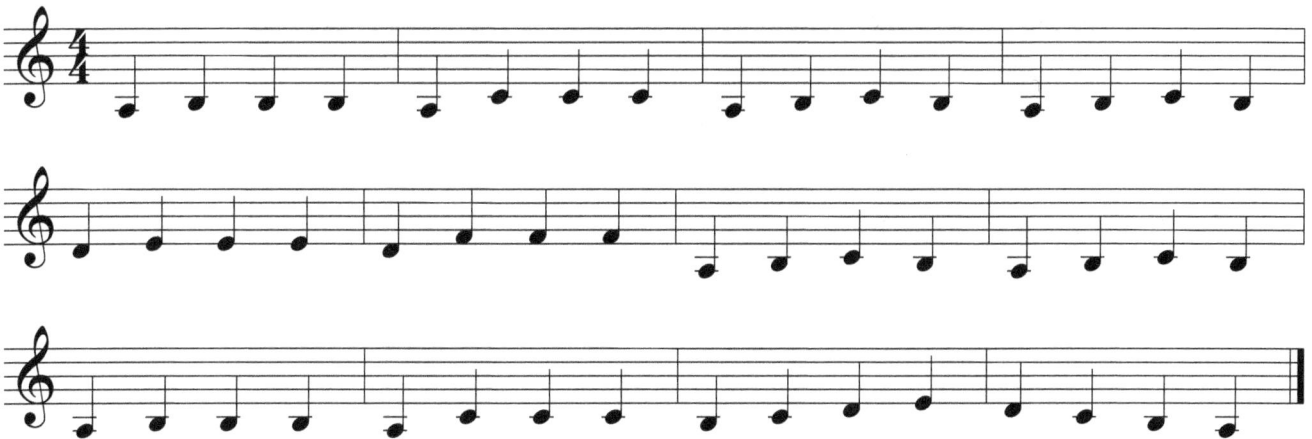

Tumbleweed

Review Strings 1 through 5

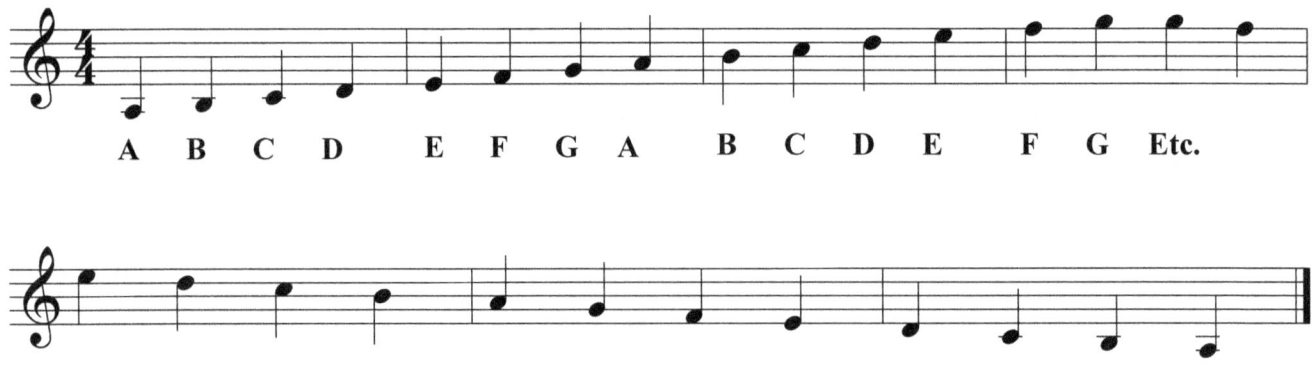

La Lune Tune

Notes on the Sixth String

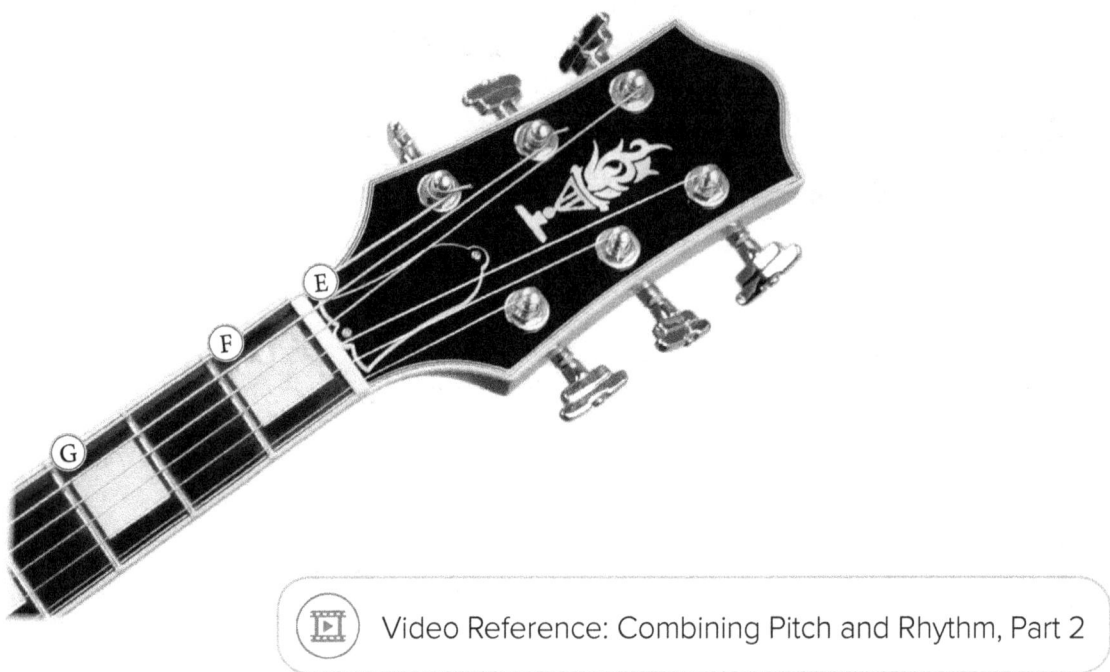

 Video Reference: Combining Pitch and Rhythm, Part 2

Play the E note on the sixth string open.

Play the F note on the sixth string first fret with the first finger.

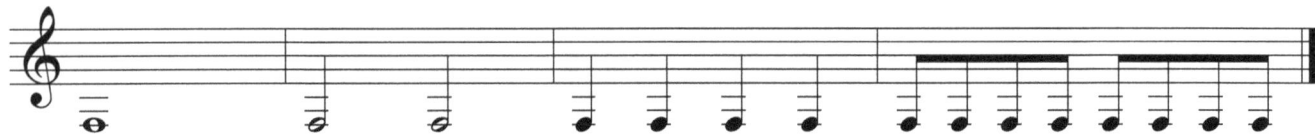

Play the G note on the sixth string third fret with the third finger.

Sixth String Practice

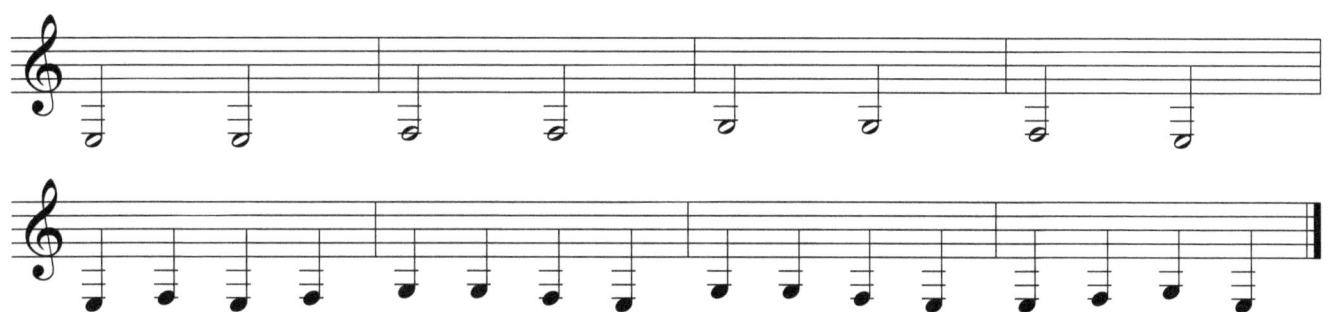

Sixth String Exercise

The following songs use only the fifth and sixth strings.

Low, Low Lydian

A Little Metal

Review all Six Strings

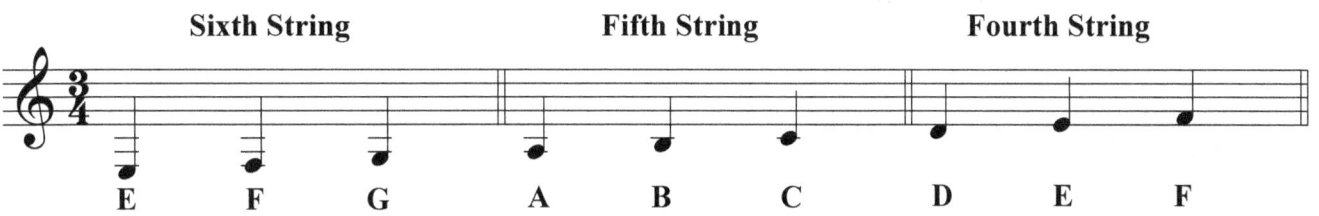

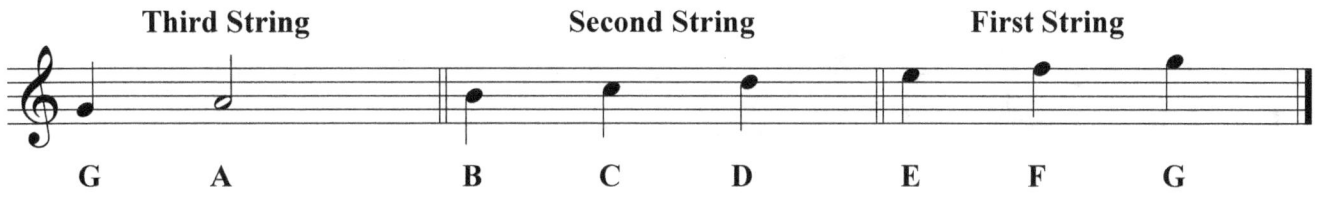

A Classic Study

A Baroque Study

 # Introducing Accidentals

The smallest distance between two notes is called a half step. To play a half step on the guitar, start anywhere on the neck, and then play a note one fret higher or lower. Playing a half step higher is called sharp (#). Playing a half step lower is called flat (♭).

Reading Sharps   Video Reference: Reading Accidentals

The note F# is played on the first string, second fret.

Notice that the sharp sign (#) is only shown once per measure. After its first appearance, all other notes of the same type (in this case the "F") are all sharp up until the bar line.

Example: Play the F# in measure 2 on the fourth string, fourth fret.

That's Sharp

Reading Flats

The note G♭ is also played on the first string, second fret. Therefore, the G♭ is the same sound as the F♯. This is called an **enharmonic equivalent**.

Example:

In this example, you will be playing the B♭, which is on the third string, third fret.

This is Flat

Reading Naturals

The natural sign (♮) cancels out a sharp or flat, returning the note to its original pitch.

Example: Play the following example, paying close attention to the accidentals.

It's Natural

Colorful

Always Wear Your Hat

Miss Moody

Sunny Side Blues

The E♭ is played on the second string, fourth fret.

Tip:

It can take a lot of practice before you feel completely comfortable with note reading. Since that's the case, too many guitar players don't develop this skill as much as they should. However, once learned well, it can be a great deal of fun and present fascinating musical challenges.

This book has provided a great place to start, but it's only the beginning. For more practice with note reading, as well as learning more about keys and how they work, be sure to check out The Missing Method for Guitar Note Reading Series. Find out more at TheMissingMethod.com.

Unit 4: Tablature

- **Understanding Tablature**
- **Practicing TAB**
- **Reading Harmonies in TAB**

Tablature

Tablature (or TAB) is the most popular way of learning new songs. It is almost as old as standard notation for stringed instruments. The advantages of TAB are that it's easy to read and allows you to figure out songs much faster than standard notation. However, there are some drawbacks. Most TABS do not include any rhythm, meaning you have to either know how the song is supposed to sound ahead of time or rely on the standard notation, when available.

Tablature shows you *where* to play, while standard notation shows you *what* to play. Therefore, both are equally valuable when learning a new song.

To read tablature, each line represents a string on the guitar. The lowest string is the bottom line, and the highest string is the top line. (See below). Numbers are placed on the lines to show you on which fret or frets to place your fingers. For example, if you see a number 1 on the first string (the top line), simply play the first fret on the first string.

The numbers on the lines represent the fret numbers.

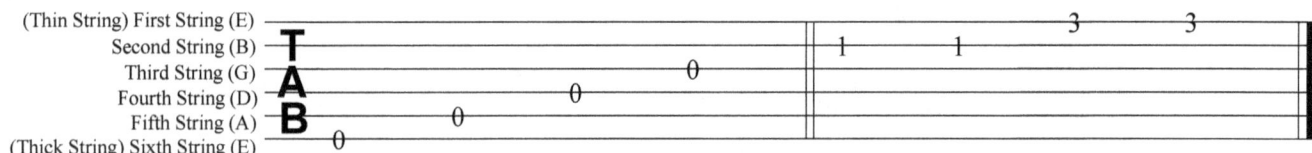

Try it: See if you can guess the name of this "happy" tune.

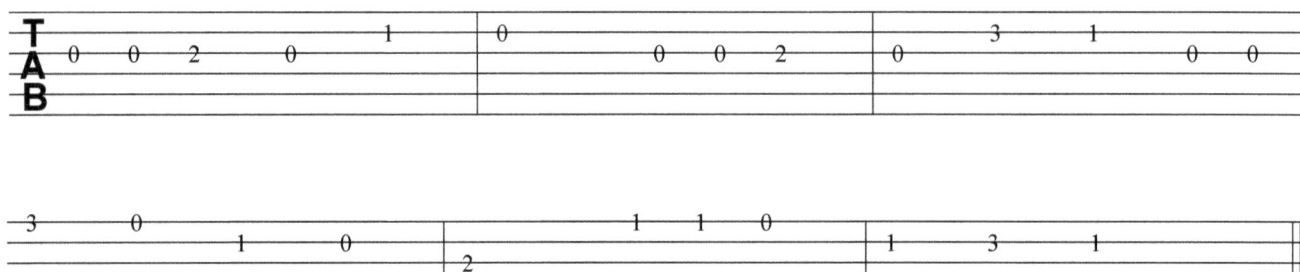

Jingle Bells

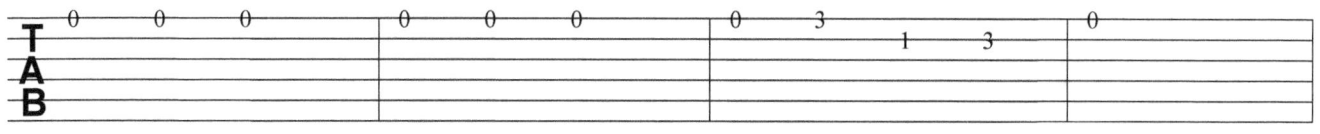

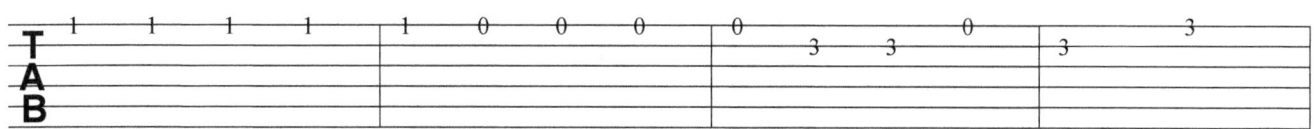

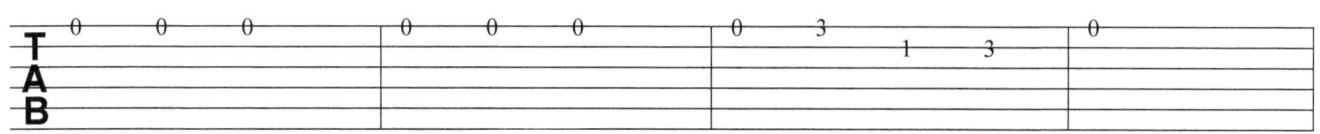

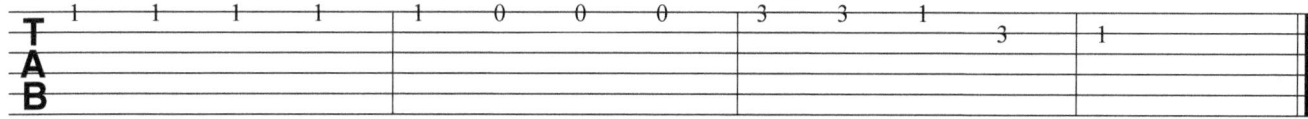

Playing more than one note at the same time

Example 1: Only play the strings with numbers on them.

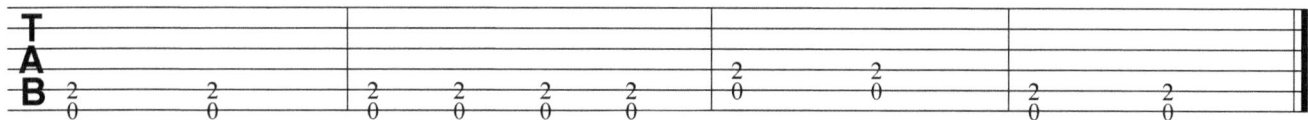

Example 2: Only strum the three strings indicated. Read each chord stack carefully.

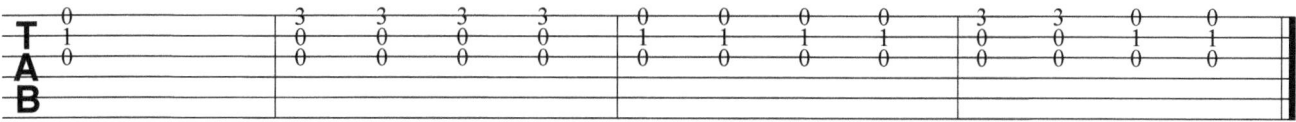

Jingle Bells
Harmonized Version

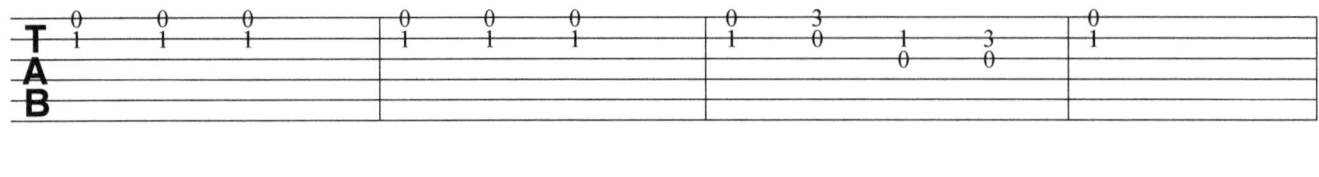

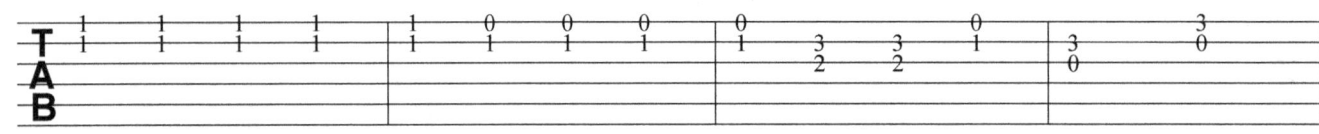

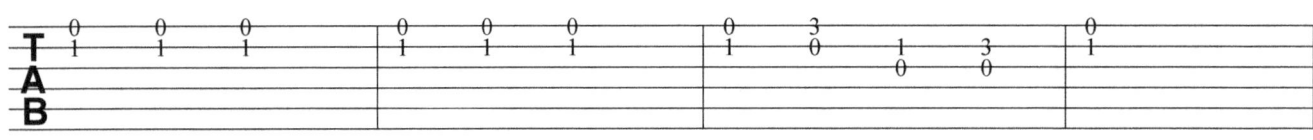

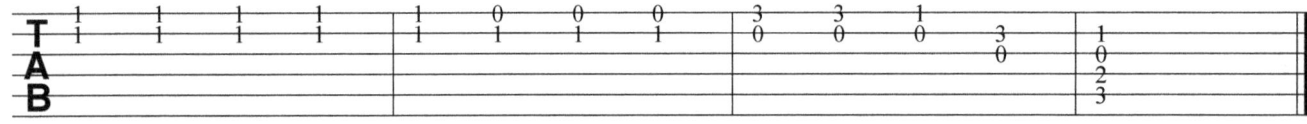

Reading TABS with full Chords

Be sure to read each chord carefully, starting from the bottom up.

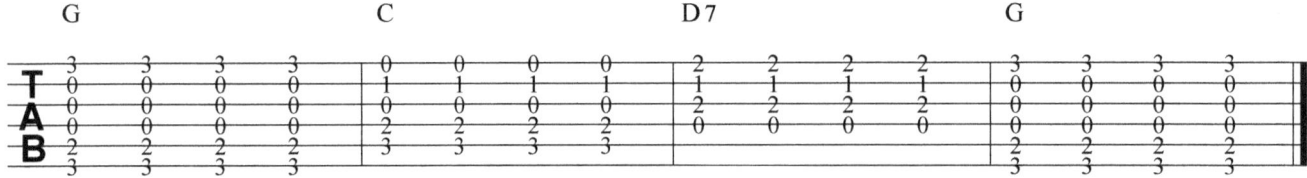

Reading TABS with Notation

When presented with TAB along with notation, you must choose which to read. One simply informs the other, but they are not meant to be played at the same time. The chord symbols above the measures show you what chords you could strum along with the song. Therefore, the chords are a separate element.

I'm On My Way

The Repeat Sign

The double dots found in the final measure is the **repeat sign**. This tells you to repeat the entire song. (See Fire Water, below). Often you will also see a reverse repeat sign at the beginning of a section with a regular repeat sign at the end of the section. This tells you to only repeat the music within that section. Below you will find examples of both.

TAB Practice Songs

Fire Water

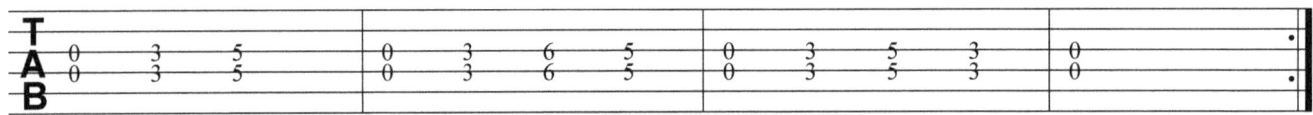

Unified Storm

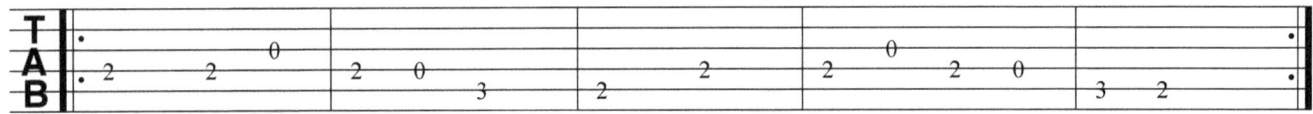

Be Yourself

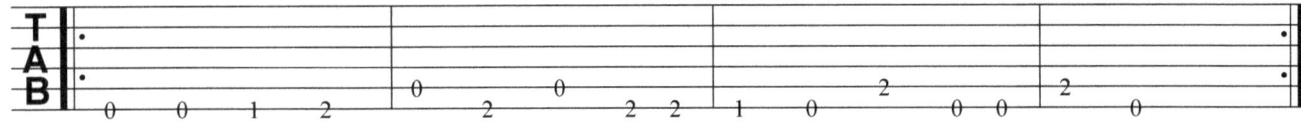

Kissing Thunder

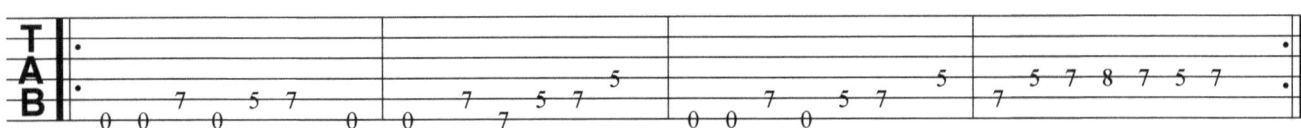

I Rather Enjoy Rock N' Roll

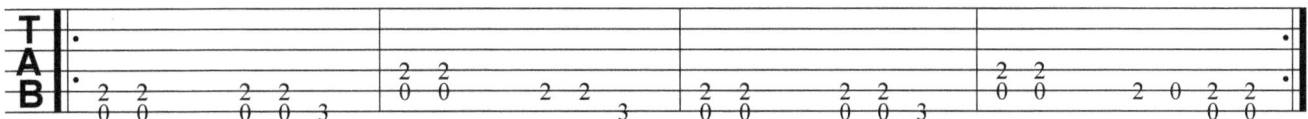

Chicago Blues Riff

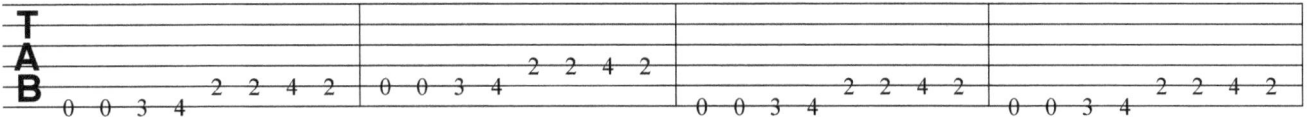

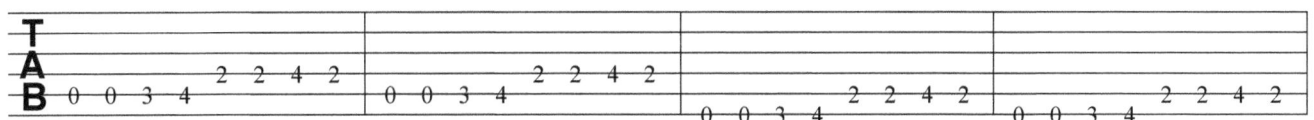

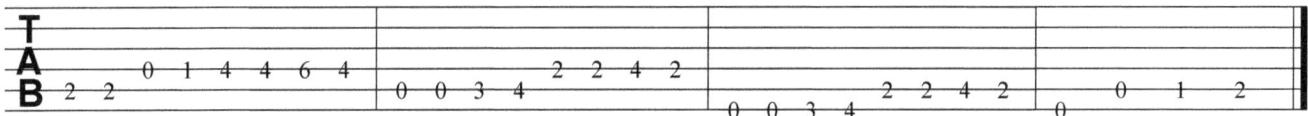

Like a Diamond

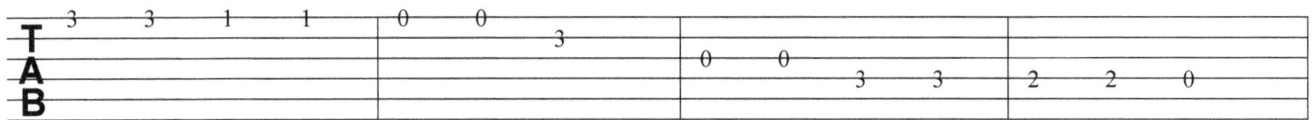

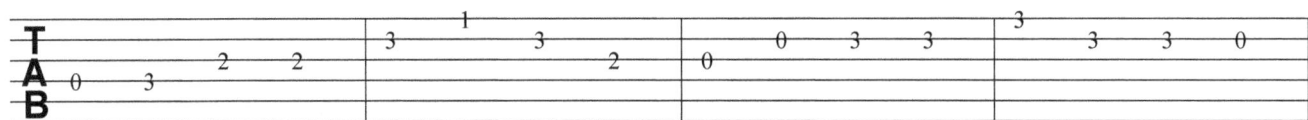

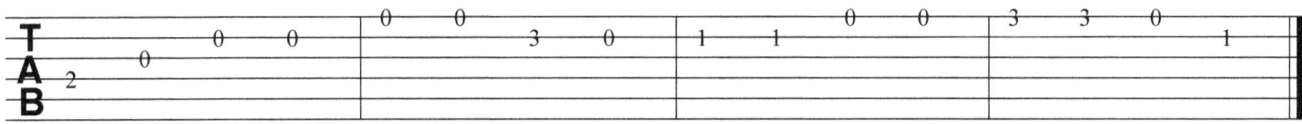

Tip:
There are lots of places online where you can find TABS for your favorite songs. To help you understand some of the symbols you will find in these songs, be sure to check out the TAB articulation chart, found in the Appendix.

Unit 5: Fingerstyle

- **The Basics of Fingerpicking**
- **Practicing Popular Patterns**
- **Travis Picking**
- **Block Chords and Double Stops**

Fingerstyle: The Basics

Fingerstyle guitar is the original way of playing the instrument. Instead of using a pick, you use your thumb and first three fingers to pluck the strings. There are many approaches to this style, ranging from classical music approaches to self-accompanied country. Here we will cover the basics of fingerstyle.

The general rule of this approach is that the thumb plays notes on the three bass strings, or strings D, A, and low E. The index finger plays the third string (G); the middle finger plays the second string (B); and the ring finger plays the first string (E).

Fingerstyle was popularized in Spain, so most of the terminology is in Spanish, including the symbols used in sheet music. Therefore, P= Pulgar (thumb); i=indice (index); m=medio (middle); and a=anular (ring finger). The pinky is not typically used in this style of playing.

Step 1: Before you try it, place all four fingers into position, meaning that each finger will be placed on their assigned string. This is something you'll always want to do before fingerpicking.

Step 2: Once you have all your fingers (including the thumb) in place, start by plucking the sixth string with the thumb, but continue to keep your other fingers on the strings.

Step 3: Next, pluck the third string with the index finger. When you do this, only move from the middle knuckle of your hand, pulling inward toward your palm, so as to minimize movement in your picking hand.

Step 4: Next, pluck the second string in the same manner, pulling your finger into your palm.

Step 5: Finally, do the same with the ring finger on the first string.

Note: Your fingers should be curved, and your wrist should NOT be lying flat. It too should be curved. Again, always prepare your fingers on the strings before playing. (See photo on opposite page.)

p = **thumb**
i = **index finger**
m = **middle finger**
a = **ring finger**

Exercise 1: Using the G chord, practice the P I M A finger pattern.

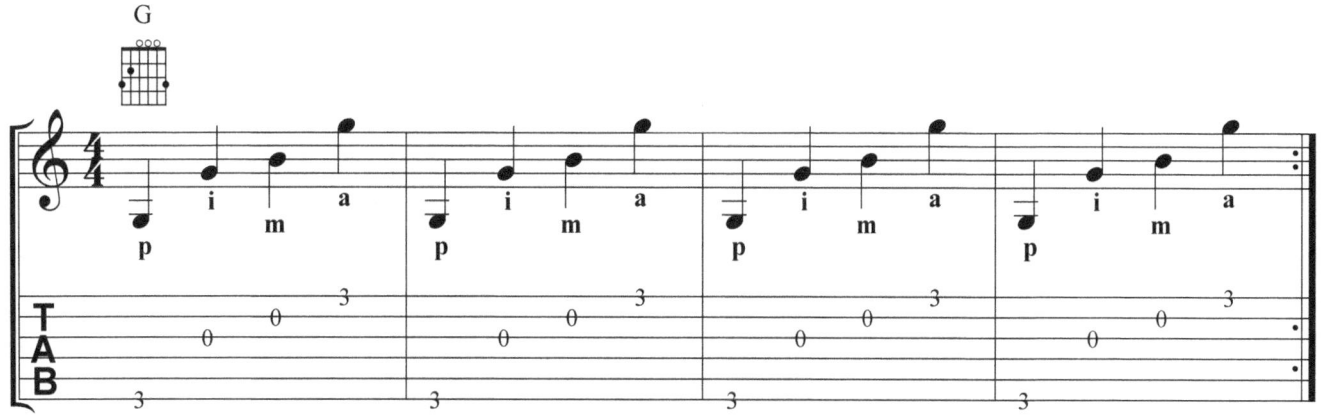

Exercise 2: Using the Am chord, practice the finger pattern starting with the fifth string instead of the sixth.

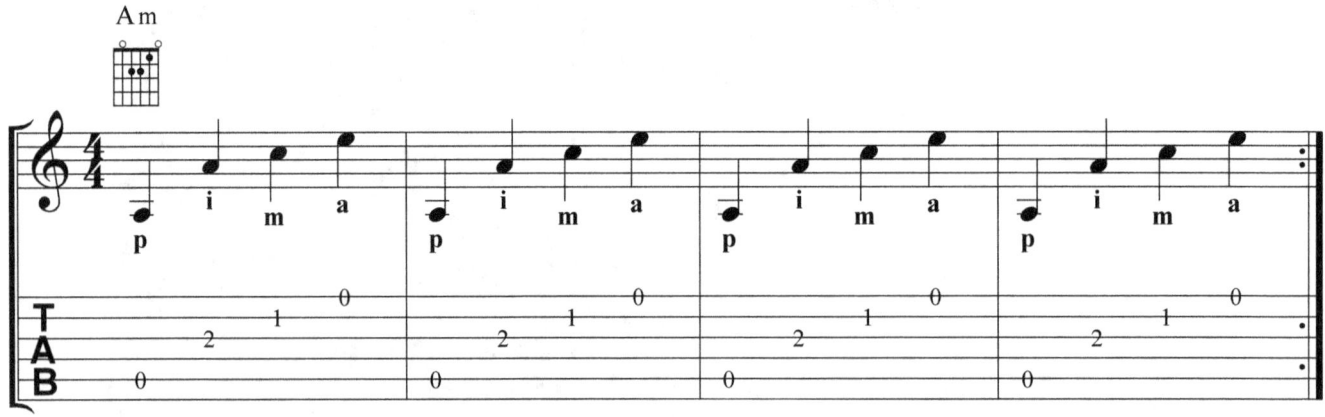

Exercise 3: Using the D chord, practice the finger pattern with the thumb plucking the fourth string.

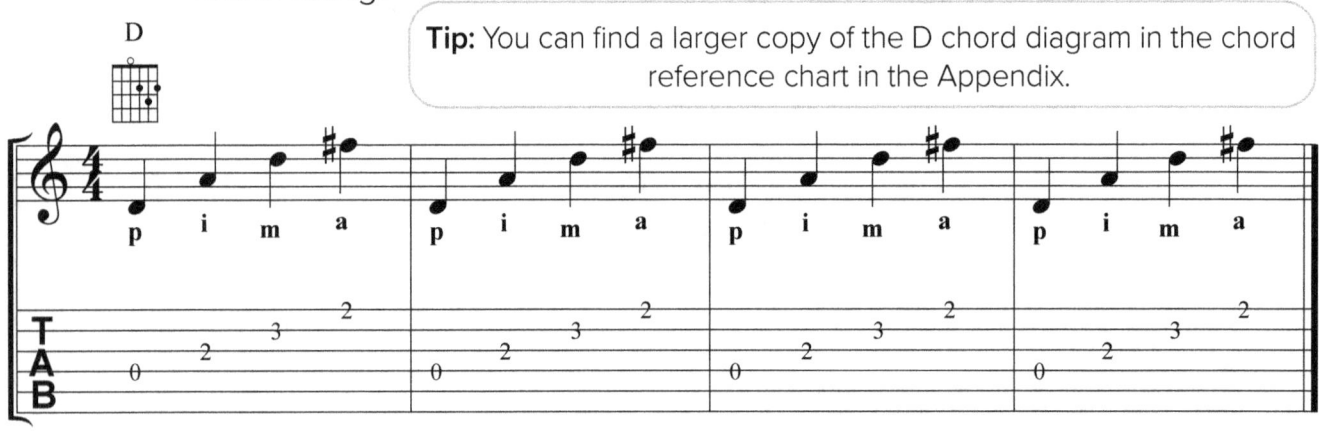

Tip: You can find a larger copy of the D chord diagram in the chord reference chart in the Appendix.

Exercise 4: Now practice changing from chord to chord.

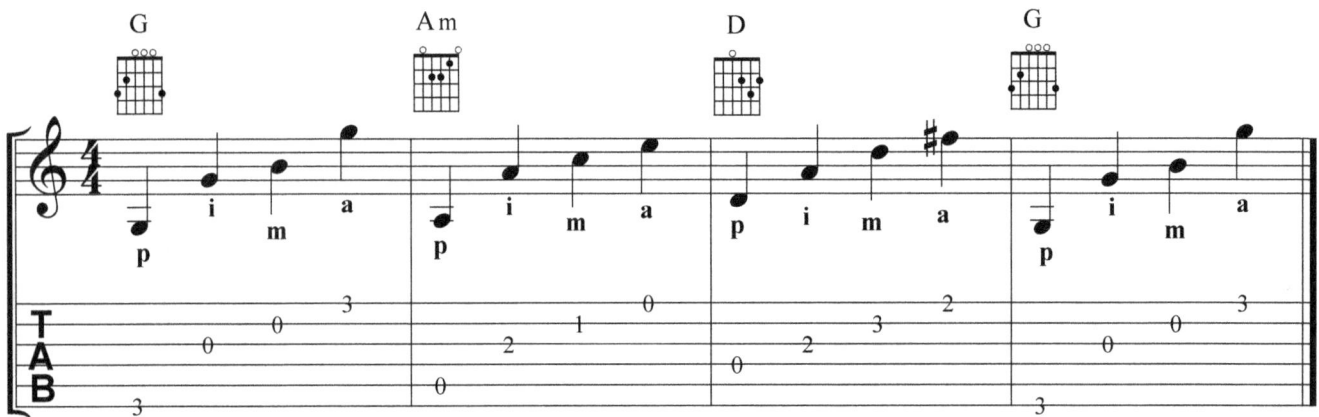

Exercise 5: Now practice the same chords with eighth notes.

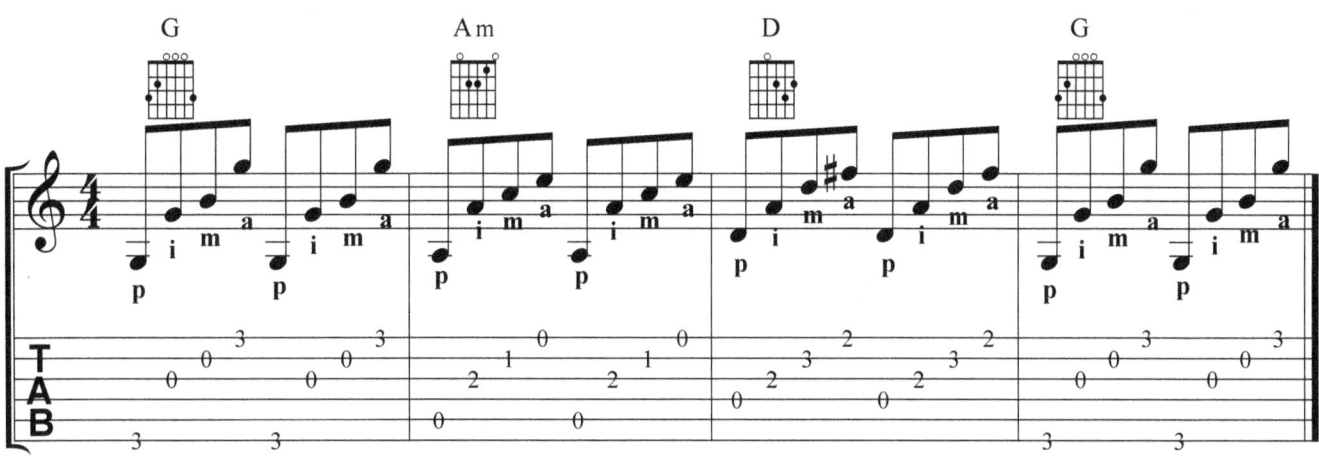

A New Pattern: P I M A M I

Exercise 1: Practice the P I M A M I finger pattern with the G chord.

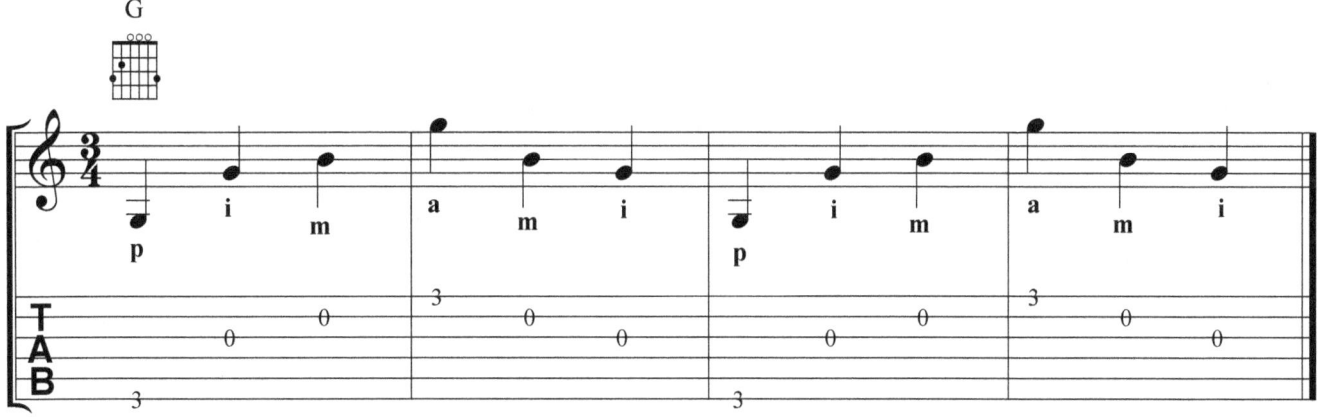

Exercise 2: Practice using the Am chord, starting with the fifth string.

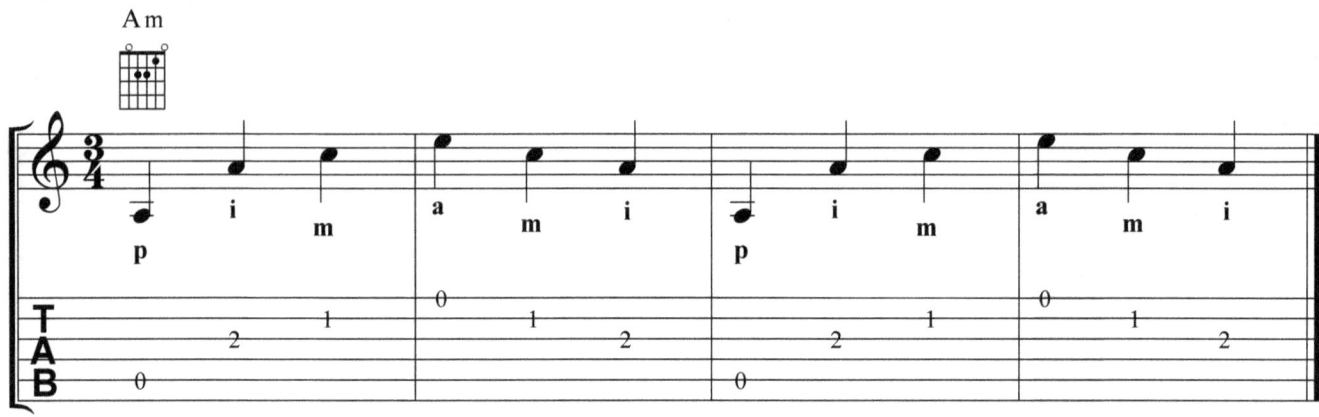

Exercise 3: Practice using the D chord, again plucking the fourth string with the thumb.

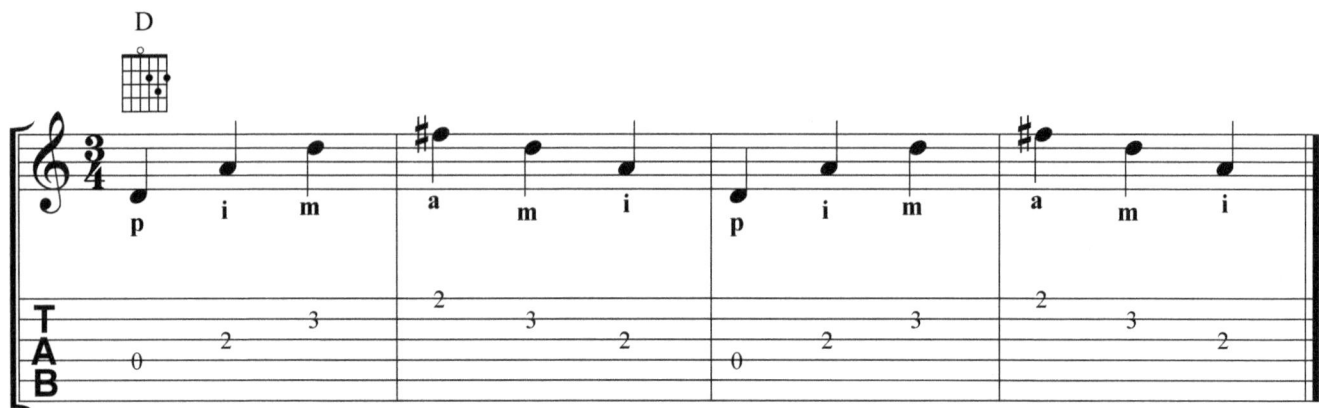

Exercise 4: Practice changing from chord to chord.

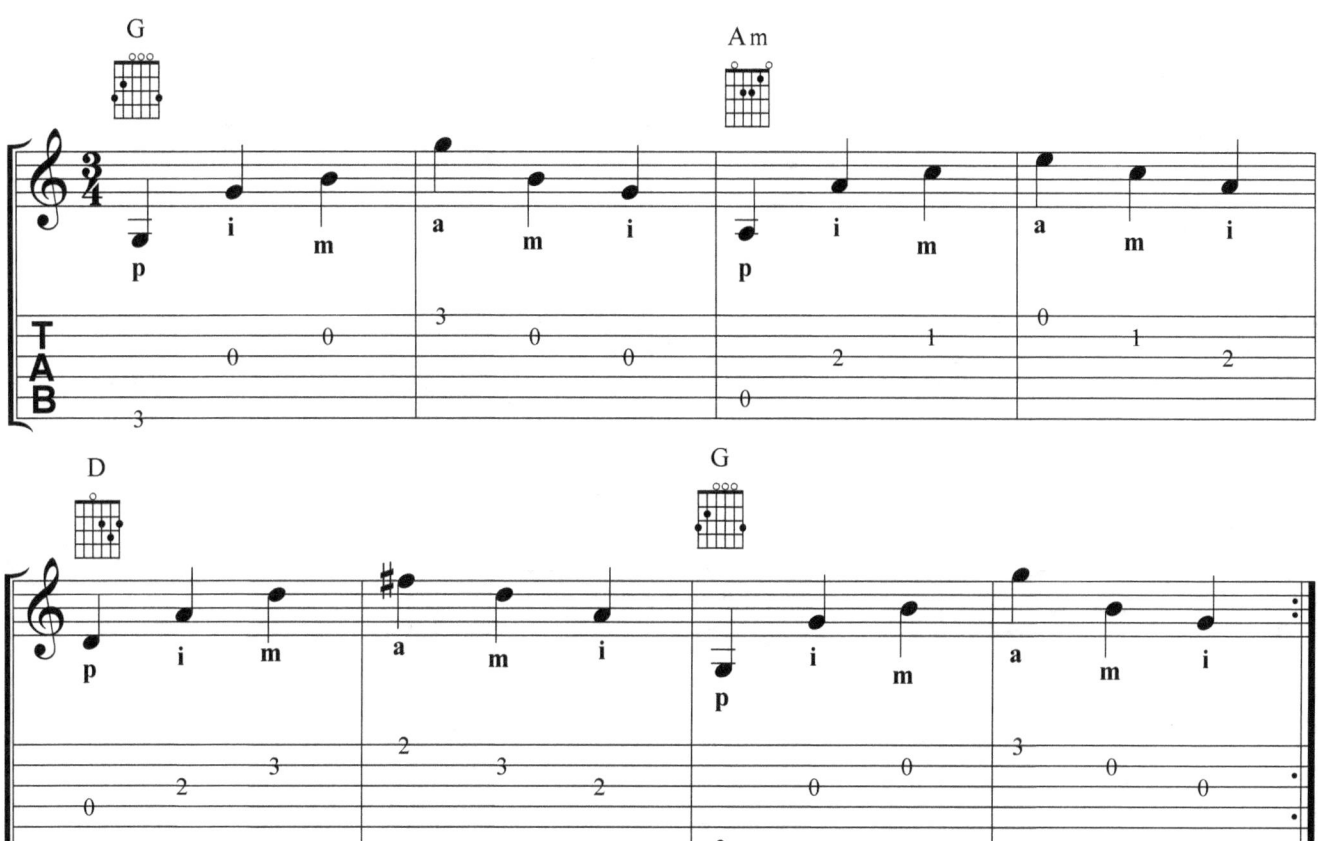

Exercise 5: Practice the same chords with eighth notes.

A New Pattern: P I M I A I M I

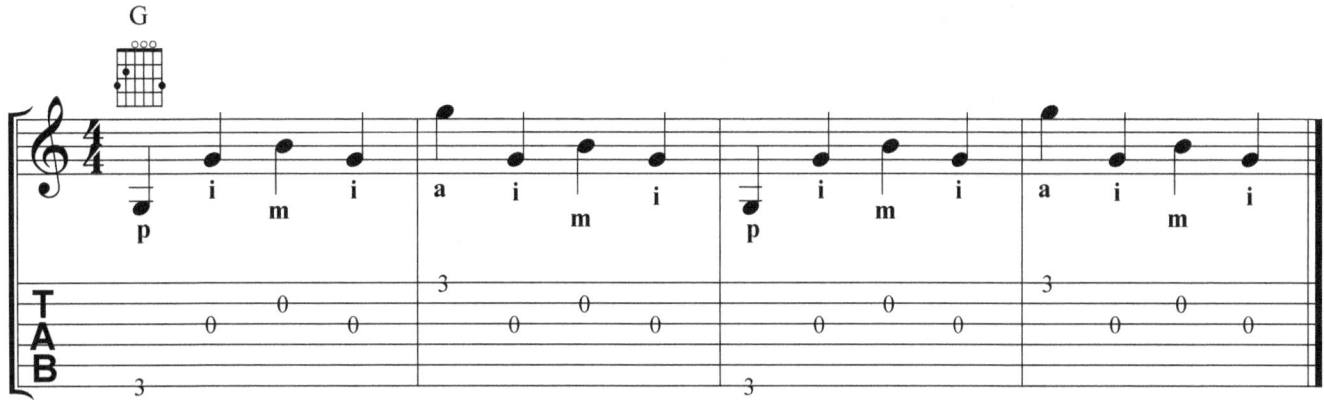

Try it: Practice P I M I A I M I with Eighth Notes

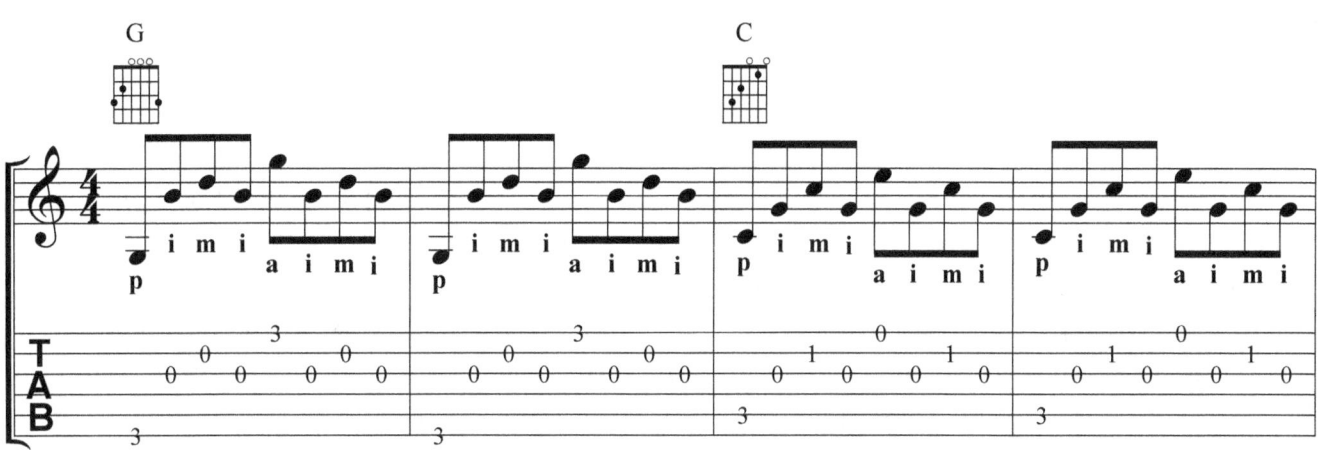

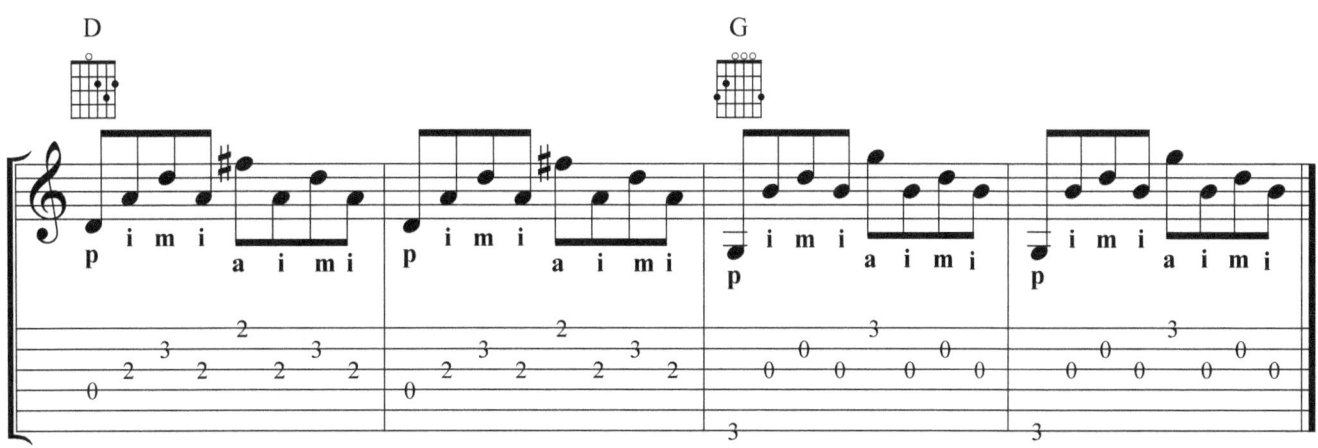

Travis Picking

Travis picking is a country style of playing named after Merle Travis, who popularized the style. It contains two defining features. The first is the bass notes. In Travis picking, the first bass note (played by the thumb) plucks the root of the chord (lowest note of the chord). The next bass note (also played by the thumb) is five notes away from the original bass note. This alternating bass line is a feature in a great deal of country music as well as other styles. The second identifying characteristic of Travis picking is a two to three note chord, often played on the downbeat of each measure. (See the examples below.)

In the next example, in order to stay consistent with the Travis picking style, it becomes necessary to include the low G note on the last string, third fret when playing the C chord. This can be achieved in one of two ways. First, you can simply remove your third finger from the low C on string five and move it over to the last string. Second, you could re-finger the C chord so that your pinky finger is placed on the low C (string 5, fret 3) and your third finger is placed on the low G (string 6, fret 3).

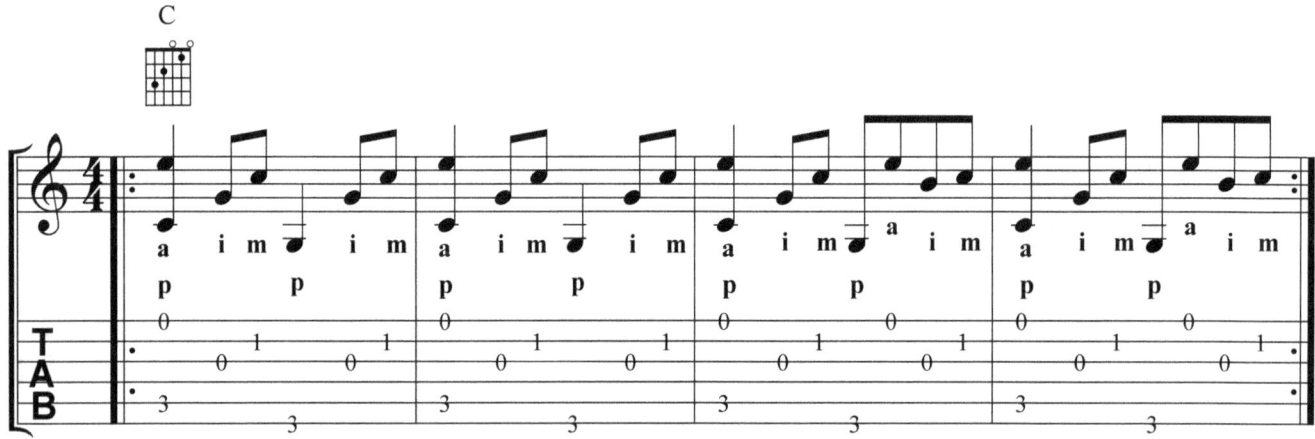

The Travis Blues

Block Chords and Double Stops

A **block chord** simply refers to playing a chord using your fingers rather than strumming with either the pick or thumb. In a block chord, each note of the chord is simultaneously plucked with your fingers. (See the example below.)

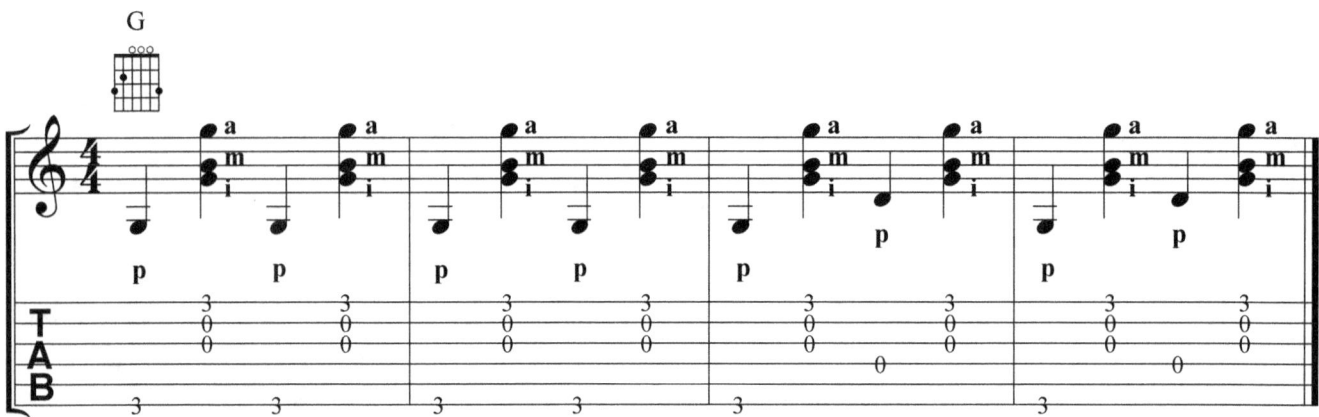

Double stops are when you play two notes at once. The term comes from traditional string instruments, like the violin, where playing two notes at once is a special effect rather than the norm, like it is on the guitar. The following examples show you common ways of performing double stops while fingerpicking.

Exercise 1: Practice the following finger combination: p a followed by i m

Exercise 2: Practice the following finger combination: p m followed by i a

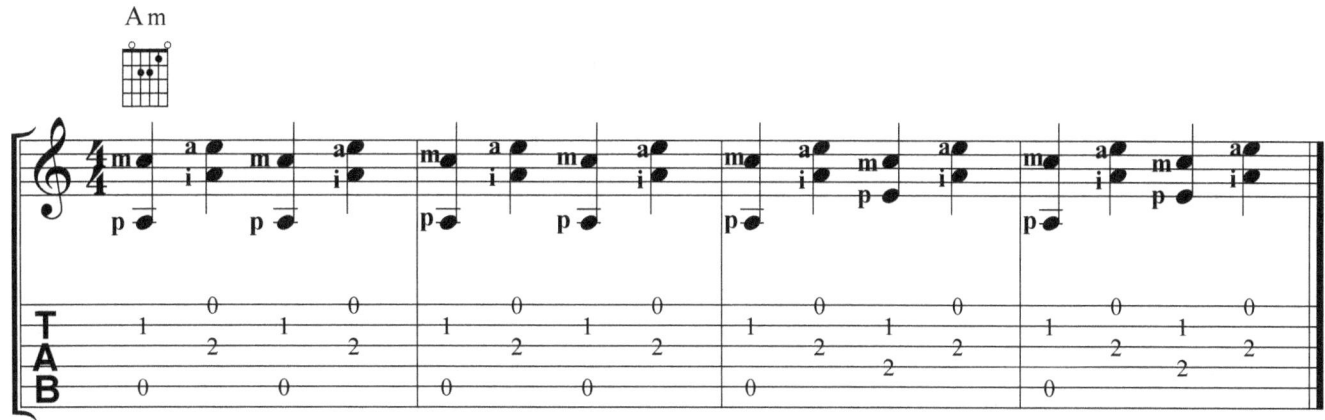

Exercise 3: Practice the following finger combination: p i followed by m a.

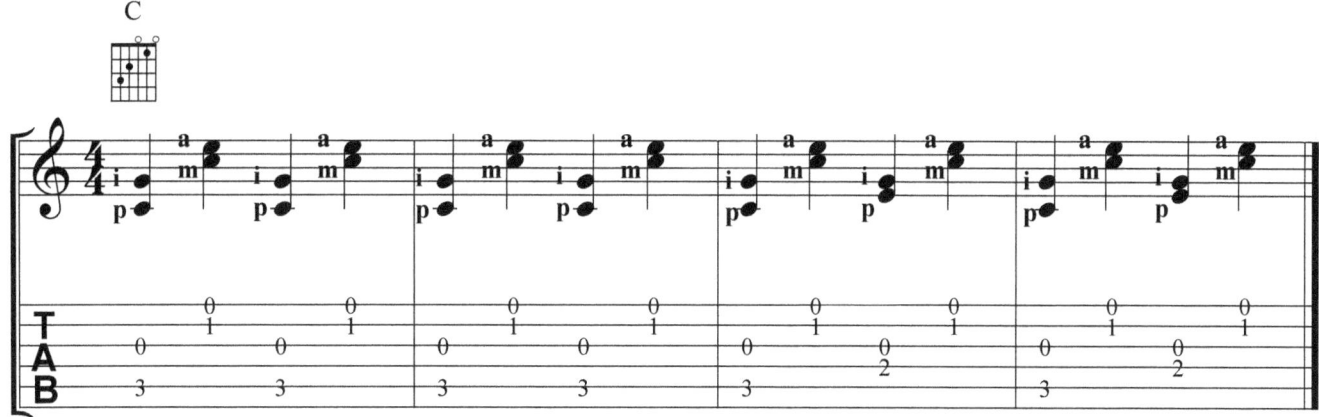

Spring Blooms

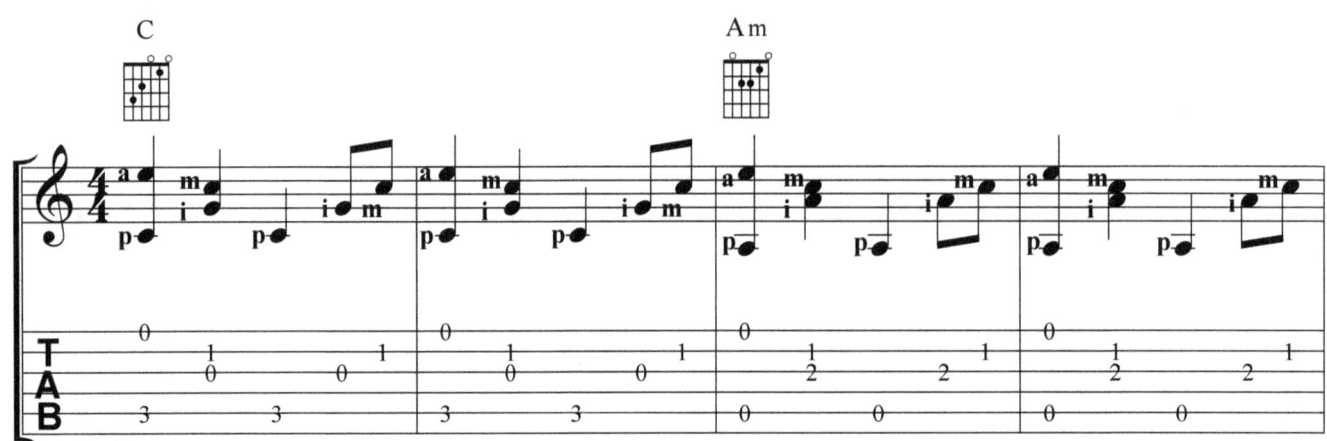
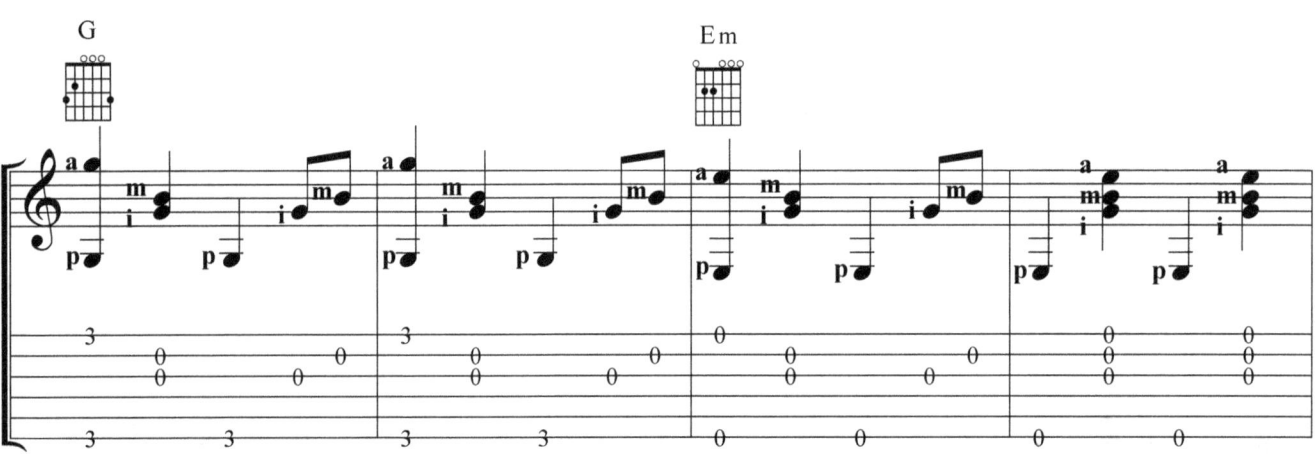
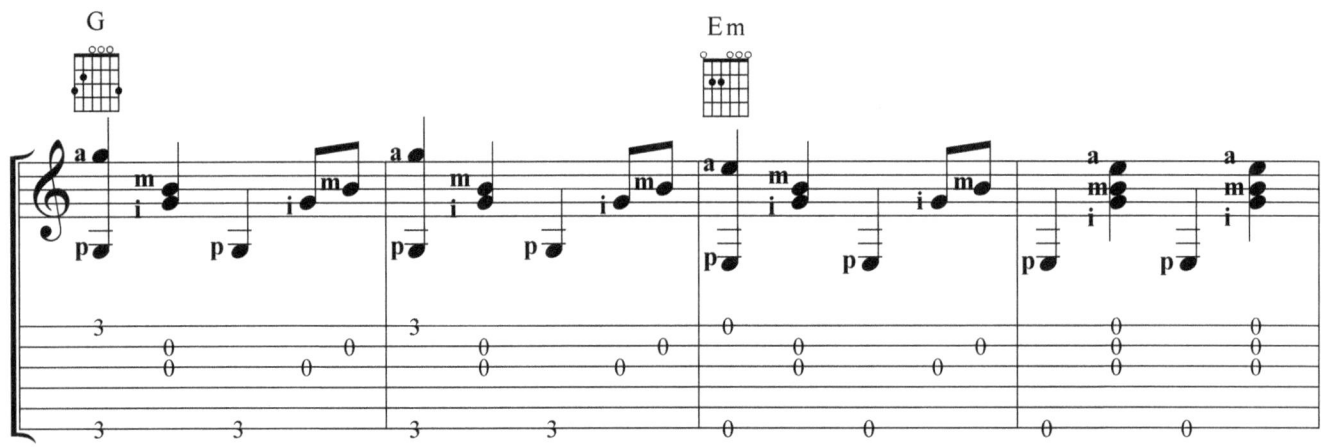

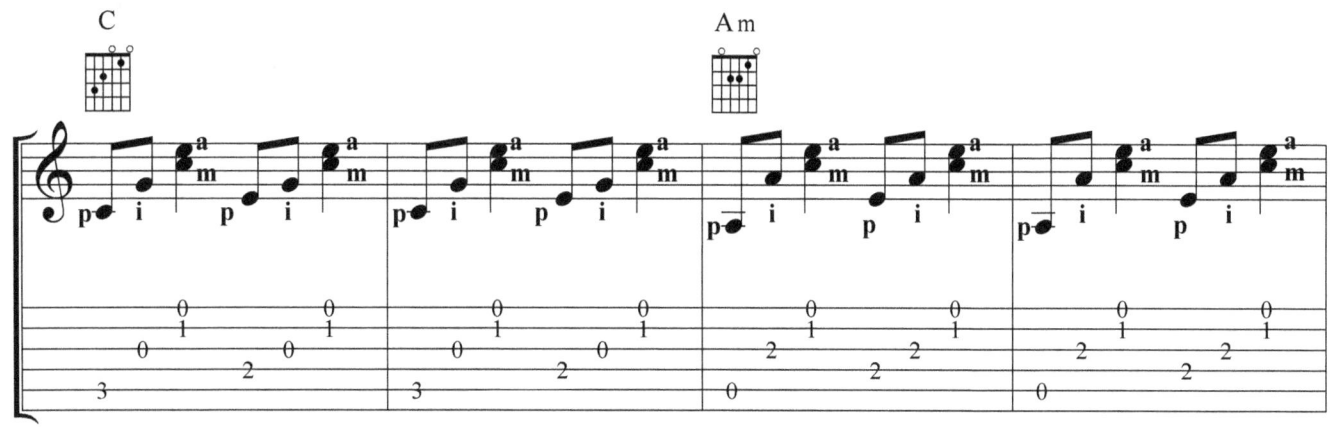
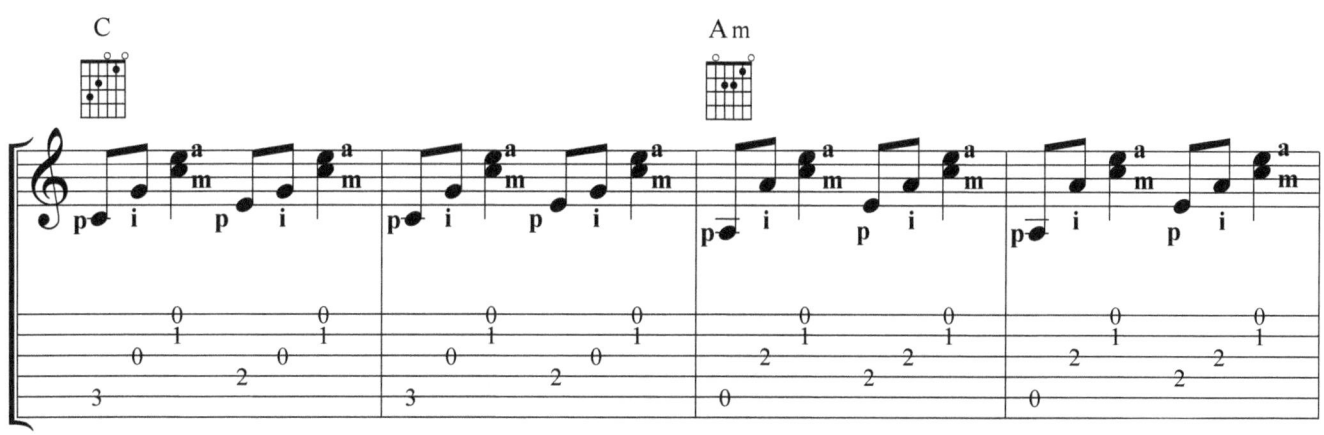
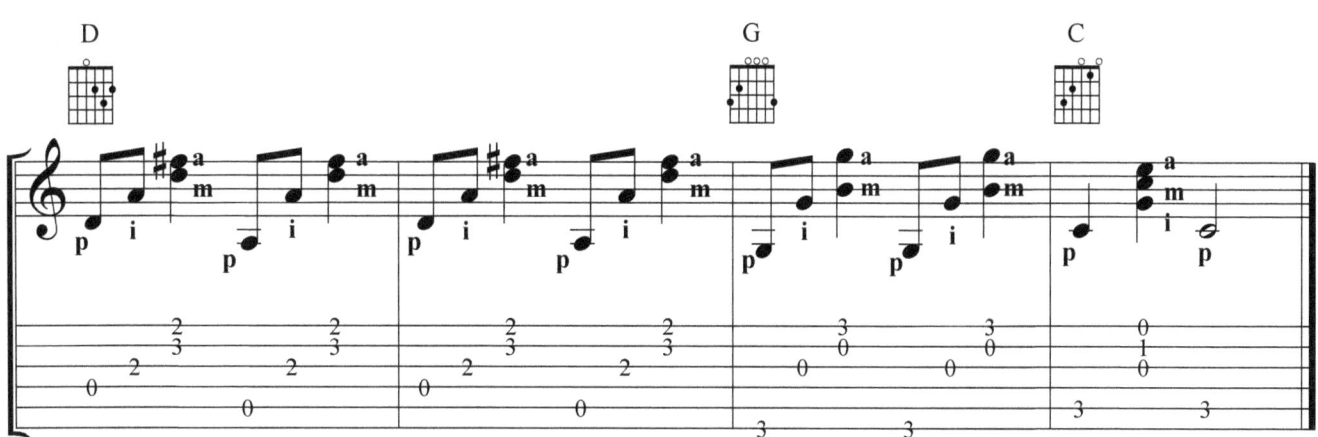

Unit 6: Power Chords

- Open Power Chords
- Root 6 Power Chords
- Root 5 Power Chords
- Combining Roots
- Palm Muting

Open Power Chords

Power chords, also known as "rock chords" are two note chords that can be played all over the neck. They are usually shown with a note name plus the number five. Like this: A5. This means that one of the two notes is A and the other is five notes away in alphabetical order. Therefore, in an A5 chord you have the notes A and E. Since the chord symbol AE would be confusing, A5 is used instead.

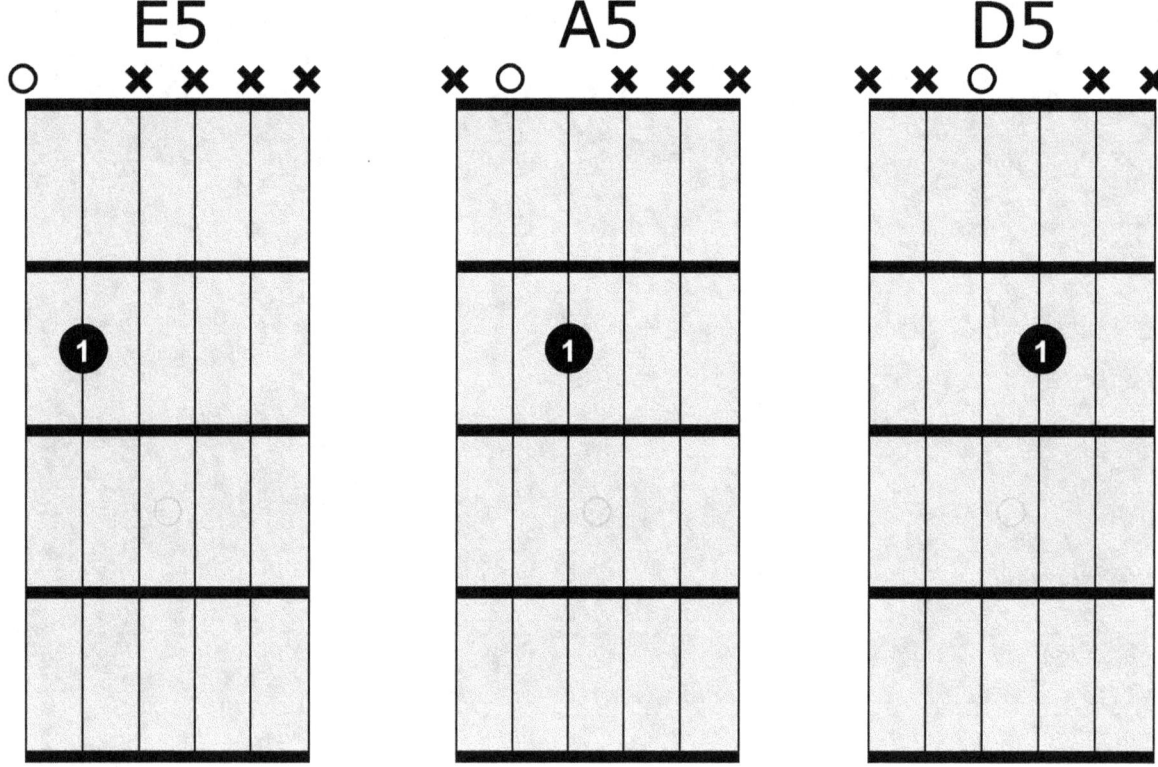

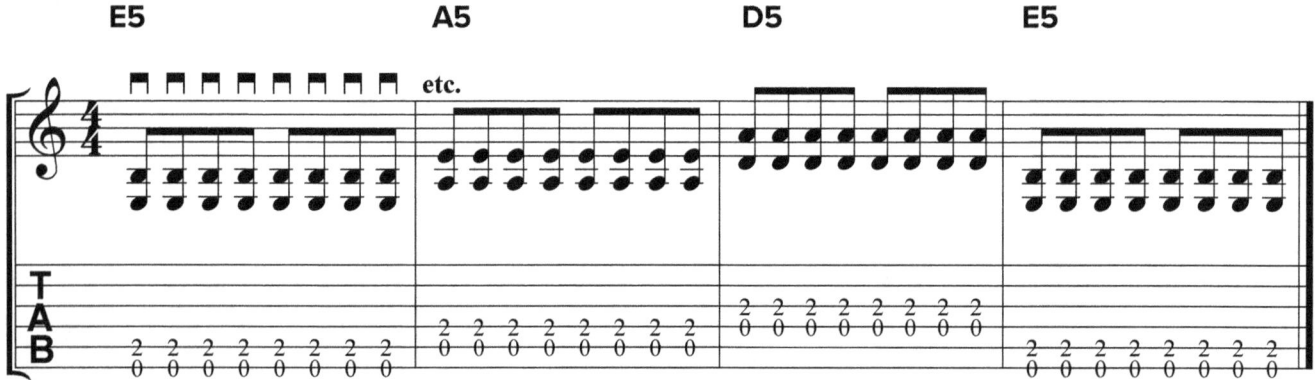

The Power of Blues

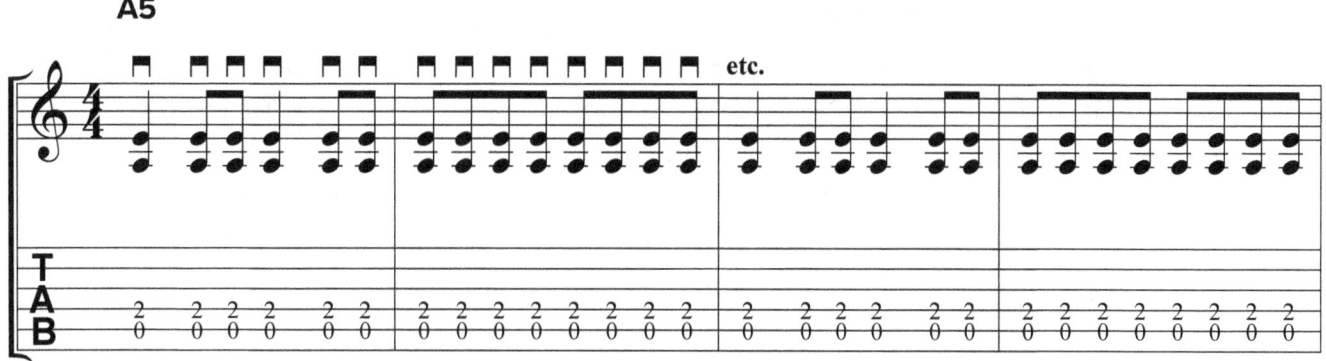
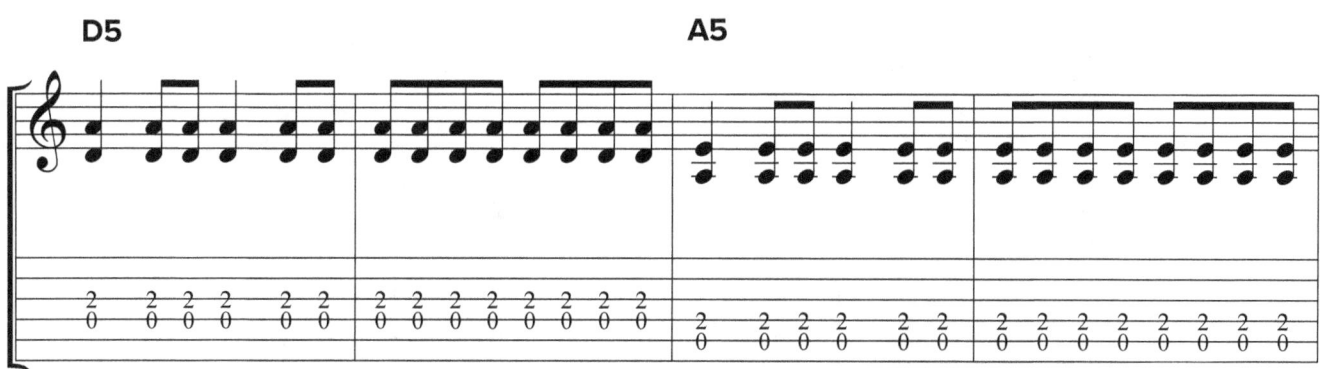
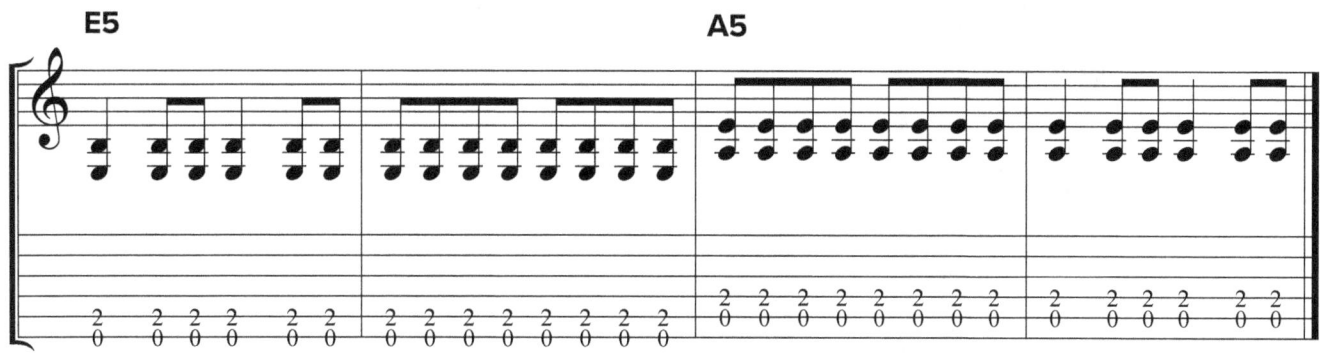

Root 6 Power Chords

Since power chords only consist of two notes, it becomes possible to play these chords easily all over the neck. To do so, take an E5 power chord. Then move the note on the second fret up by a half step. Next, place your index finger on the first fret of the last string. This chord shape is the F5 power chord. This shape can be moved up the string. As you move, each new place on the neck will become a new power chord. The chart below shows you the natural notes on the sixth string, which are the roots of the power chords. Therefore, if you take the F5 shape (shown below) and move it up to the third fret, the resulting chord is a G5 power chord.

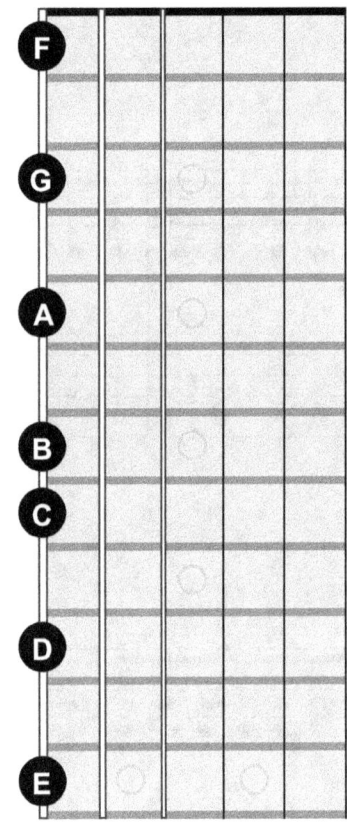
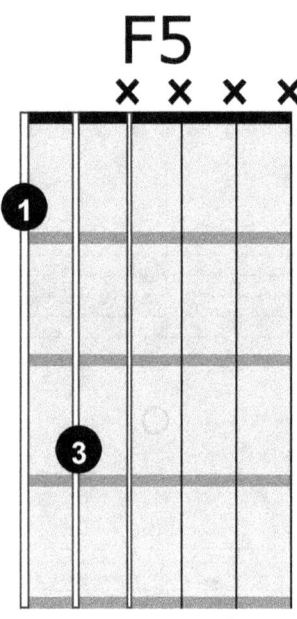

Exercise 1: E5, F5, and G5

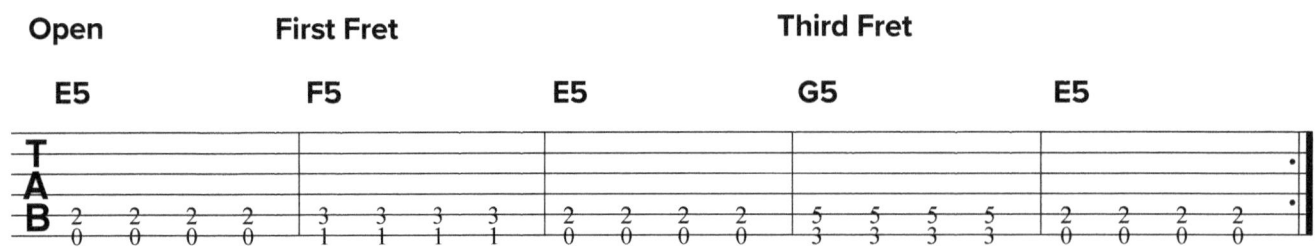

Exercise 2: G5, A5, and B5

```
    G5              A5              B5              A5              G5
T|---------------|---------------|---------------|---------------|---------------||
A|---------------|---------------|---------------|---------------|---------------||
B|-5--5--5--5----|-7--7--7--7----|-9--9--9--9----|-7--7--7--7----|-5--5--5--5----||
  3  3  3  3     5  5  5  5     7  7  7  7     5  5  5  5     3  3  3  3
```

Exercise 3: B5, C5, and A5

```
    B5              C5              B5              C5              A5
T|---------------|---------------|---------------|---------------|---------------||
A|---------------|---------------|---------------|---------------|---------------||
B|-9--9--9--9----|-10-10-10-10---|-9--9--9--9----|-10-10-10-10---|-7--7--7--7----||
  7  7  7  7     8  8  8  8     7  7  7  7     8  8  8  8     5  5  5  5
```

Exercise 4: C5, D5, and E5

```
    C5              D5              E5              D5              E5    C5
T|---------------|---------------|---------------|---------------|---------------||
A|---------------|---------------|---------------|---------------|---------------||
B|-10-10-10-10---|-12-12-12-12---|-14-14-14-14---|-12-12-12-12---|-14-14-10-10---||
  8  8  8  8     10 10 10 10    12 12 12 12    10 10 10 10    12 12 8  8
```

Exercise 5: Review

```
    E5      D5      C5      B5      A5      G5      F5      E5
T|-------------------|-------------------|-------------------|-------------------||
A|-------------------|-------------------|-------------------|-------------------||
B|-14--14--12--12----|-10--10--9---9-----|-7---7---5---5-----|-3---3---2---2-----||
  12  12  10  10     8   8   7   7      5   5   3   3      1   1   0   0
```

Exercise 6: Review

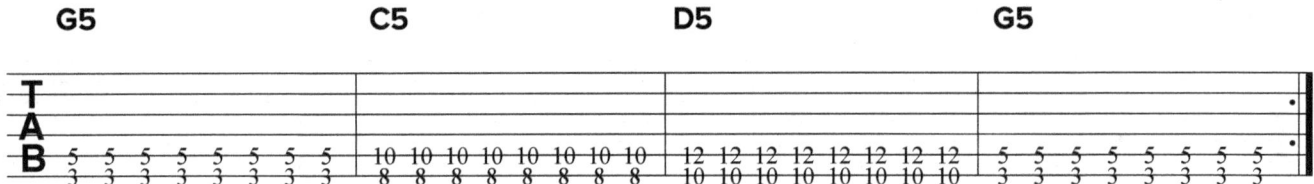

Exercise 7: F#5 and Review

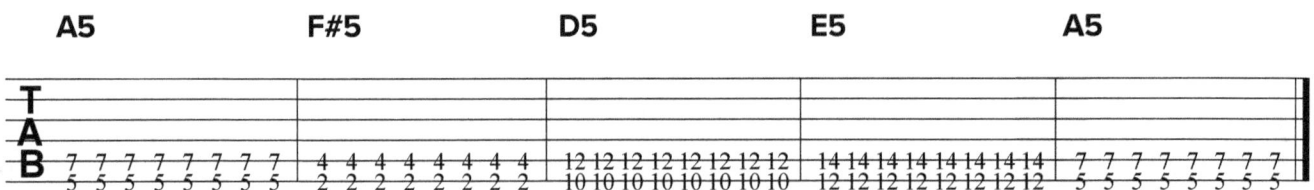

Exercise 8: Review

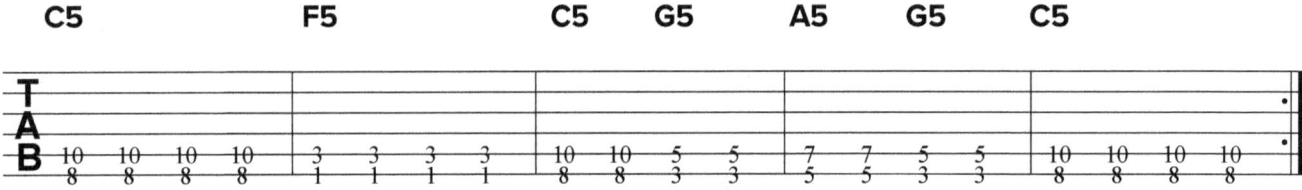

Exercise 9: Review

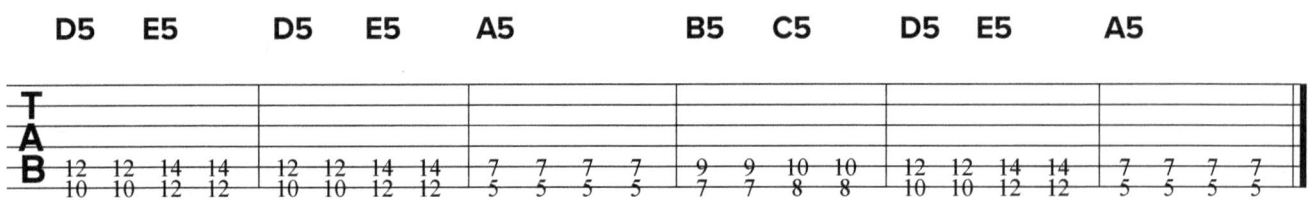

Root 5 Power Chords

Root 5 power chords work in the same manner as the root 6. However, with this set of chords, since the root of the chord is on the fifth string, the sixth string is not played. Also note that the first natural note on this string is the B natural, found on the second fret of the fifth string.

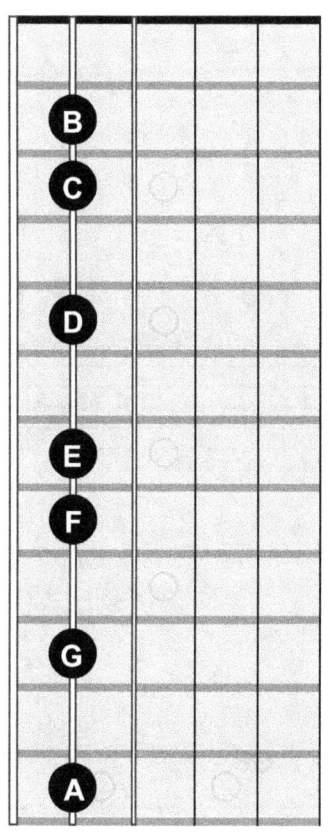
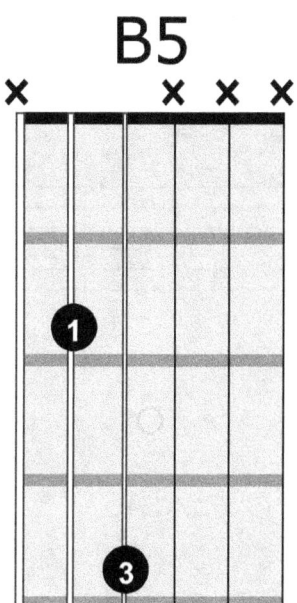

Exercise 1: A5, B5, and C5

Open	2nd Fret	3rd Fret		
A5	B5	C5	B5	A5

Exercise 2: C5, D5, and E5

C5	D5	E5	D5	C5

```
T|------------------|------------------|------------------|------------------|------------------||
A|--5--5--5--5------|--7--7--7--7------|--9--9--9--9------|--7--7--7--7------|--5--5--5--5------||
B|--3--3--3--3------|--5--5--5--5------|--7--7--7--7------|--5--5--5--5------|--3--3--3--3------||
```

Exercise 3: E5, F5, and G5

E5	F5	G5	F5	E5

```
T|------------------|------------------------|------------------------|------------------------|------------------||
A|--9--9--9--9------|--10--10--10--10--------|--12--12--12--12--------|--10--10--10--10--------|--9--9--9--9------||
B|--7--7--7--7------|--8---8---8---8---------|--10--10--10--10--------|--8---8---8---8---------|--7--7--7--7------||
```

Exercise 4: F5, G5, and A5

F5	G5	A5	G5	F5

```
T|------------------------|------------------------|------------------------|------------------------|------------------------||
A|--10--10--10--10--------|--12--12--12--12--------|--14--14--14--14--------|--12--12--12--12--------|--10--10--10--10--------||
B|--8---8---8---8---------|--10--10--10--10--------|--12--12--12--12--------|--10--10--10--10--------|--8---8---8---8---------||
```

Exercise 5: Review

A5	G5	F5	E5	D5	C5	B5	A5

```
T|--------------------|----------------|--------------|------------|----------||
A|--14--14--12--12----|--10--10--9--9--|--7--7--5--5--|--4--4--2--2|----------||
B|--12--12--10--10----|--8---8---7--7--|--5--5--3--3--|--2--2--0--0|----------||
```

Exercise 6: Review

| C5 | F5 | G5 | C5 |

```
T|------------------|------------------------|------------------------|------------------|
A|-5-5-5-5-5-5-5-5--|-10-10-10-10-10-10-10-10|-12-12-12-12-12-12-12-12|-5-5-5-5-5-5-5-5--|
B|-3-3-3-3-3-3-3-3--|--8--8--8--8--8--8--8--8|-10-10-10-10-10-10-10-10|-3-3-3-3-3-3-3-3--|
```

Exercise 7: Review

| D5 | B5 | G5 | A5 | D5 |

```
T|------------------|------------------|------------------------|------------------------|------------------|
A|-7-7-7-7-7-7-7-7--|-4-4-4-4-4-4-4-4--|-12-12-12-12-12-12-12-12|-14-14-14-14-14-14-14-14|-7-7-7-7-7-7-7-7--|
B|-5-5-5-5-5-5-5-5--|-2-2-2-2-2-2-2-2--|-10-10-10-10-10-10-10-10|-12-12-12-12-12-12-12-12|-5-5-5-5-5-5-5-5--|
```

Exercise 8: Review

| E5 | F5 | E5 | D5 | C5 | B5 | A5 |

```
T|----------|-----------------|----------|----------|----------|----------|----------|
A|-9-9-9-9--|-10-10--9---9----|-7-7-7-7--|-5-5-5-5--|-4-4-4-4--|-2-2-2-2--|----------|
B|-7-7-7-7--|--8--8--7---7----|-5-5-5-5--|-3-3-3-3--|-2-2-2-2--|-0-0-0-0--|----------|
```

Exercise 9: Review

| B5 | Bb5 | A5 | D5 | E5 | A5 |

```
T|:-----------------------:|----------|----------|----------|
A|:-4--4--3--3--2-2-2-2---:|-7-7-7-7--|-9-9-9-9--|-2-2-2-2--|
B|:-2--2--1--1--0-0-0-0---:|-5-5-5-5--|-7-7-7-7--|-0-0-0-0--|
```

Combining Roots

Exercise 1

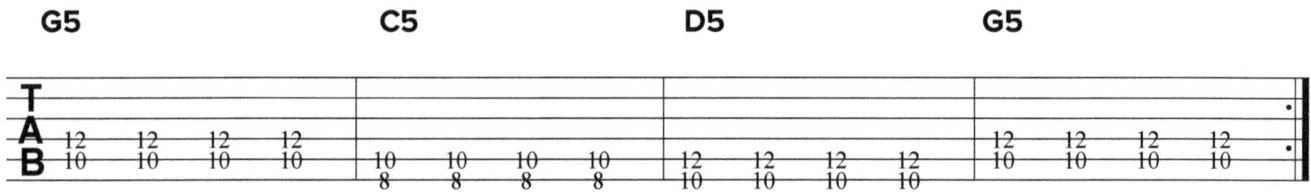

Exercise 2

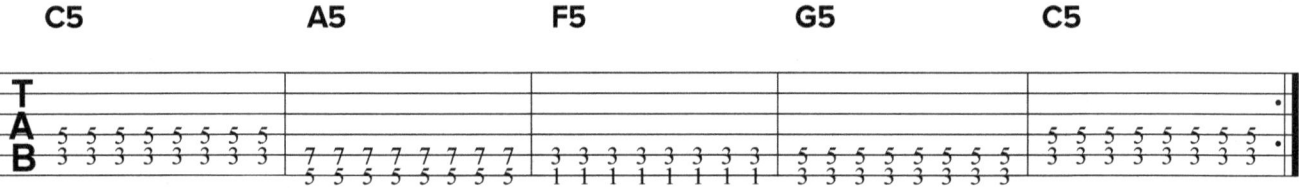

Exercise 3

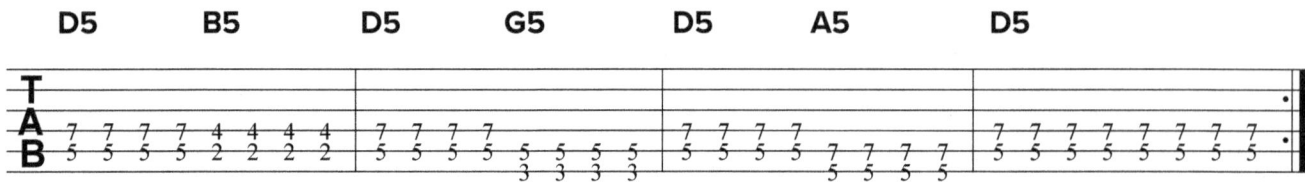

Exercise 4

Exercise 5

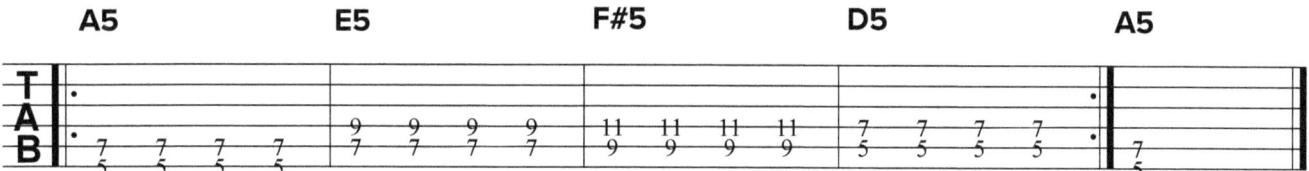

Exercise 6

Exercise 7

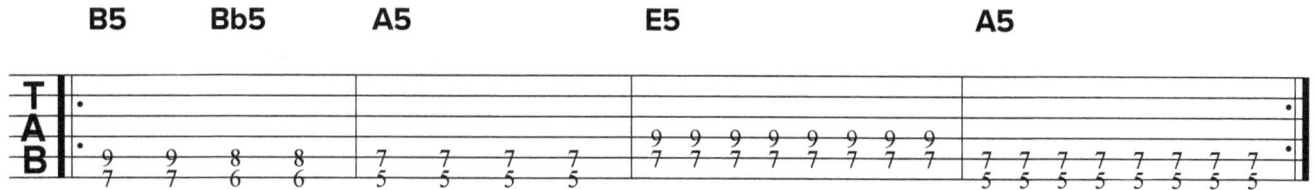

Exercise 8

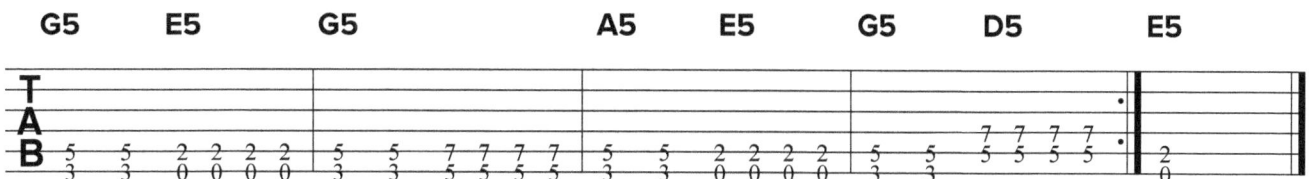

Three Note Power Chords

So far, we've practiced two note power chords. However, it is also common to include an additional string (as seen in the example below). This new note is actually the root one octave higher, so even though you are playing three notes, two of them are the same pitch in different octaves. Use the pinky finger to play the additional note.

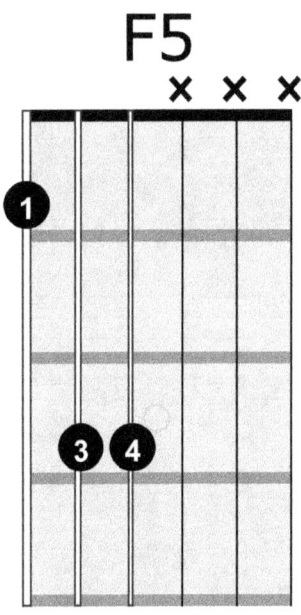

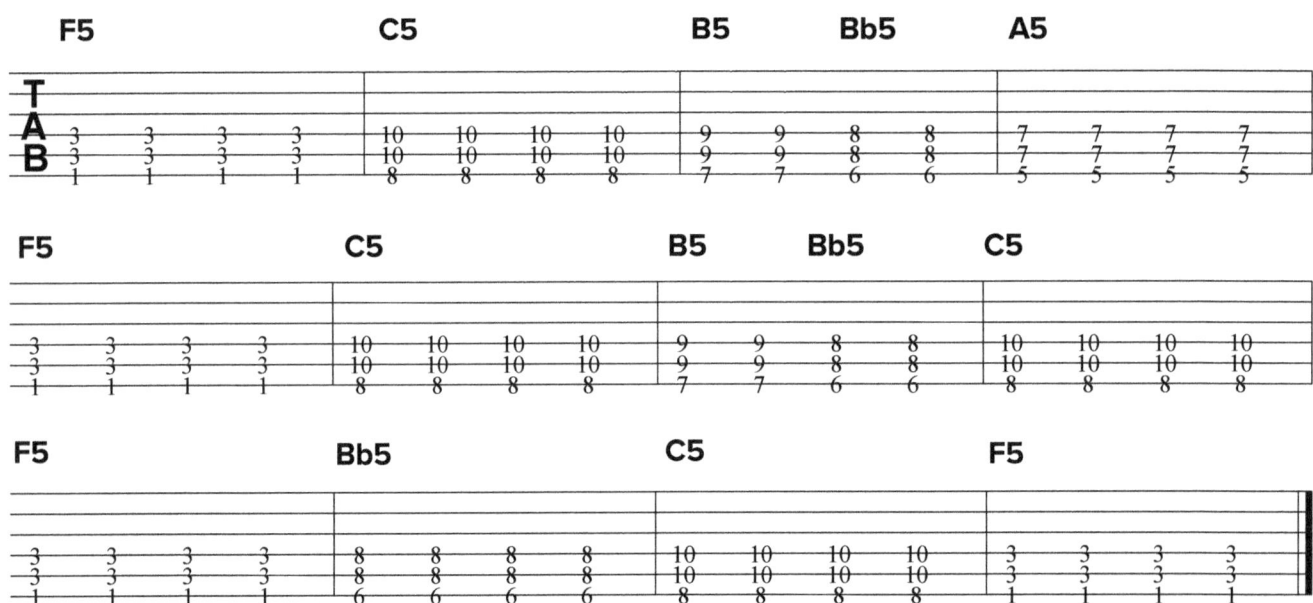

Rollin' and Rockin'

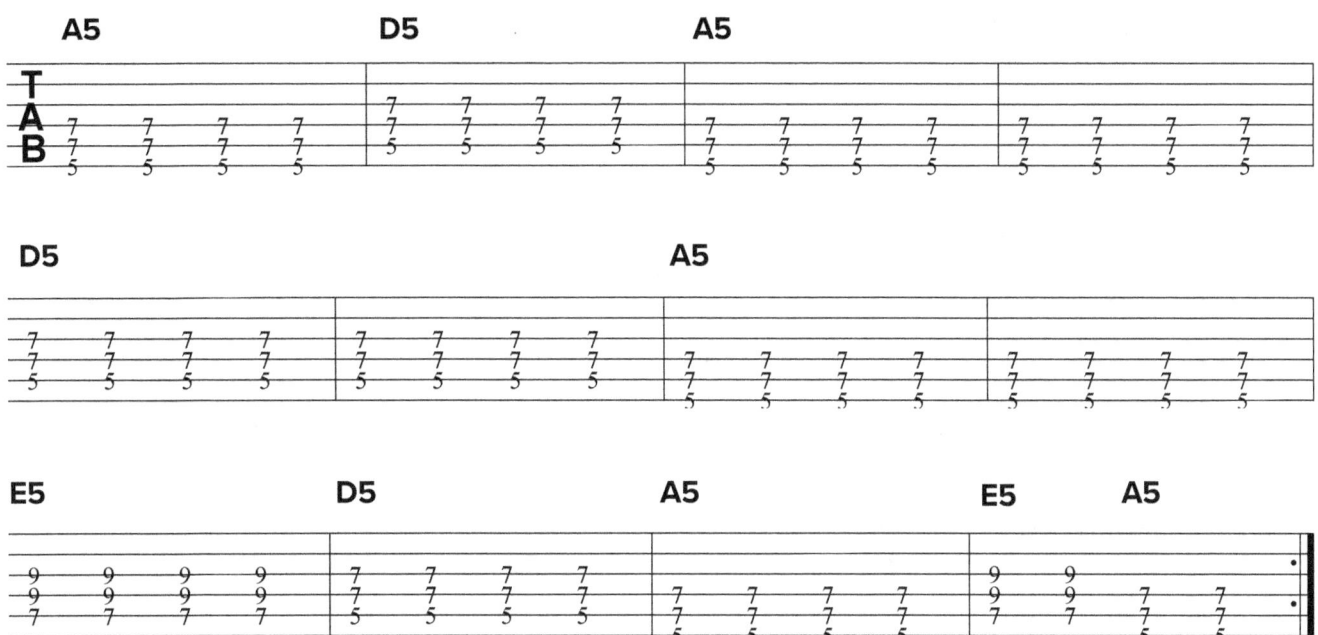

Gravestone Moon

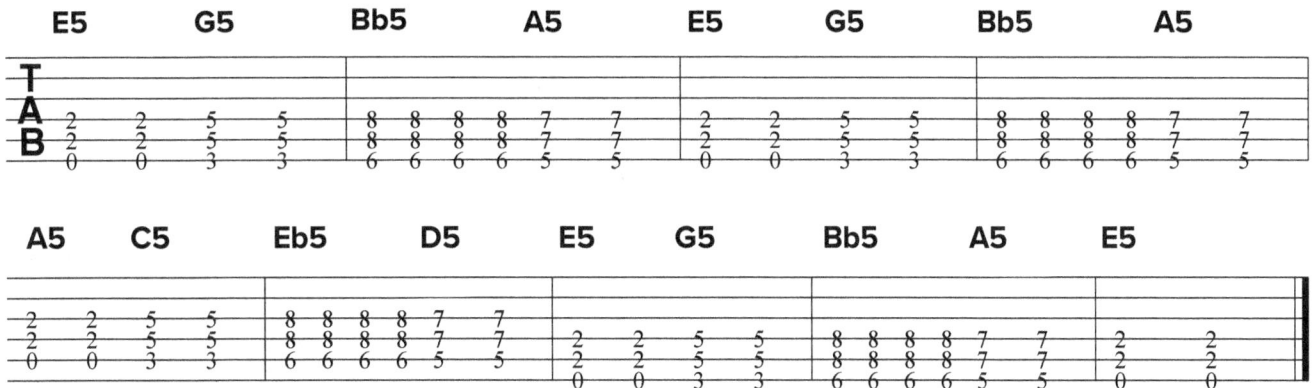

Palm Muting

Palm Muting is a technique that allows you to muffle the sound of the guitar to add variety to your playing. It is a common practice used in just about every style of music, but most often heard in all the various forms of rock. Though it is just as often used on single notes, palm muting is often associated with power chords.

To palm mute: place the heel of your hand just over the bridge so that it rests on the strings. Don't press down, just let it rest there. Keeping the heel of your hand resting on the strings, pluck the sixth string. You should still hear a sound, but one that is quieter and more muffled that before. If you don't hear this, move your hand closer to the bridge.

When to palm mute: In musical scores (TAB or traditional notation) the letters p.m. will be shown under the measure that is intended to be palm muted. Usually a dashed line will also be included to show you for how long they want you to continue palm muting. (See the example below).

Palm Mute Example

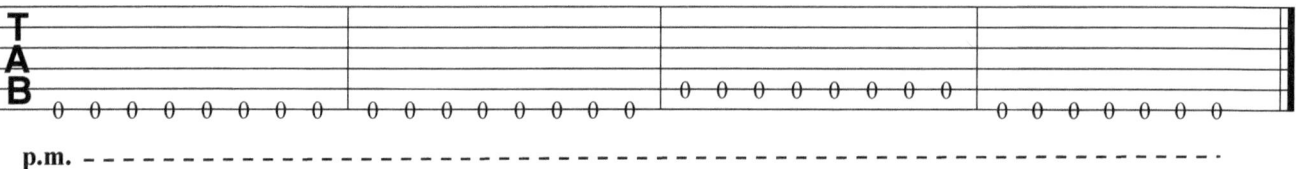

Green and Mean

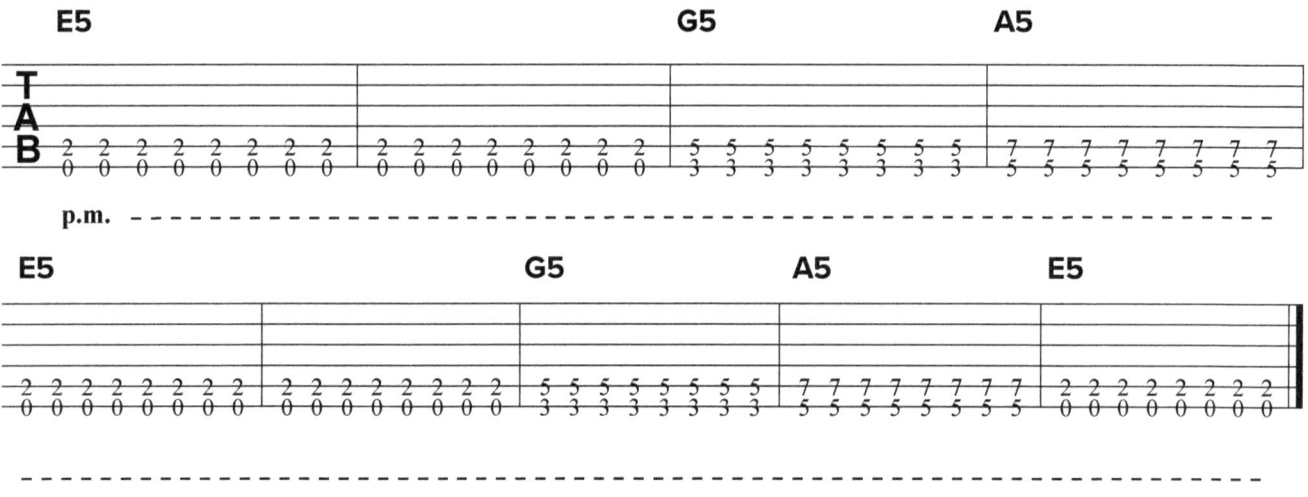

This next song includes palm muted single notes, two-note power chords (also palm muted), and three note power chords (not palm muted). Be sure to read carefully.

The War Machine

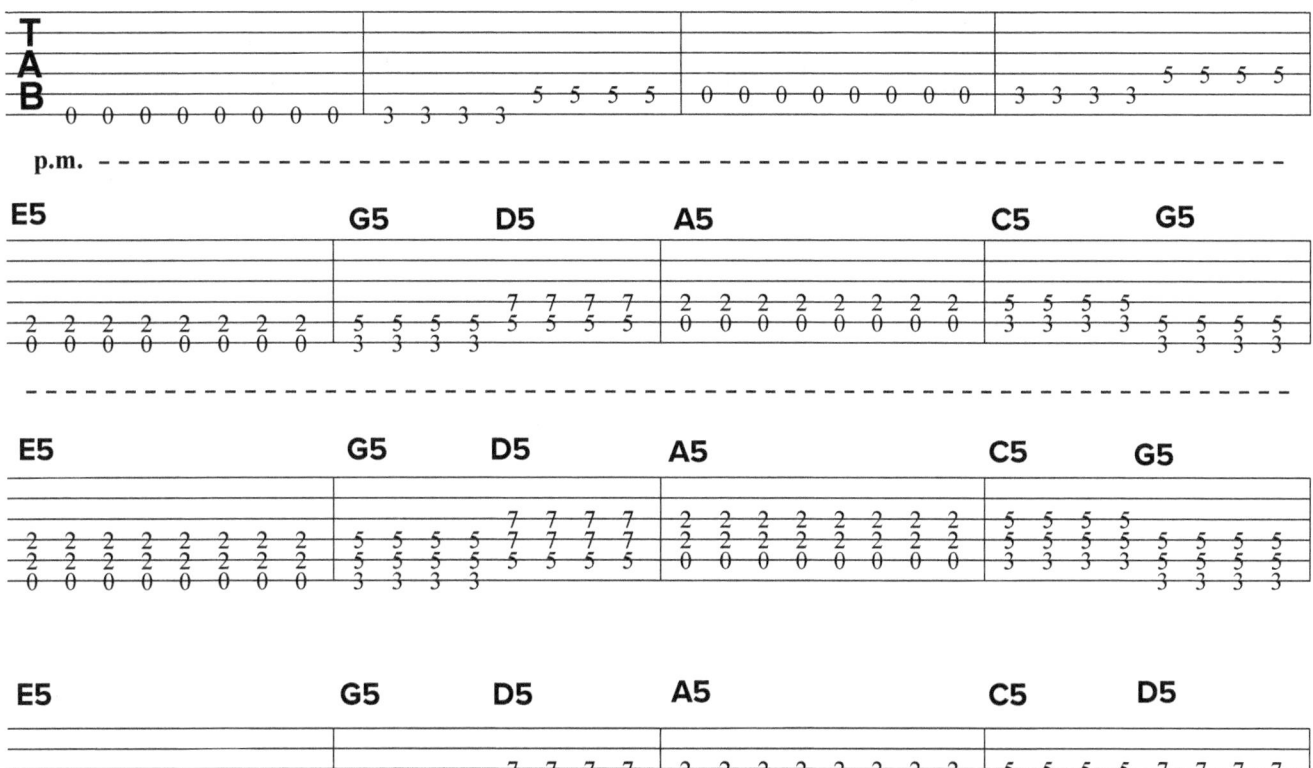

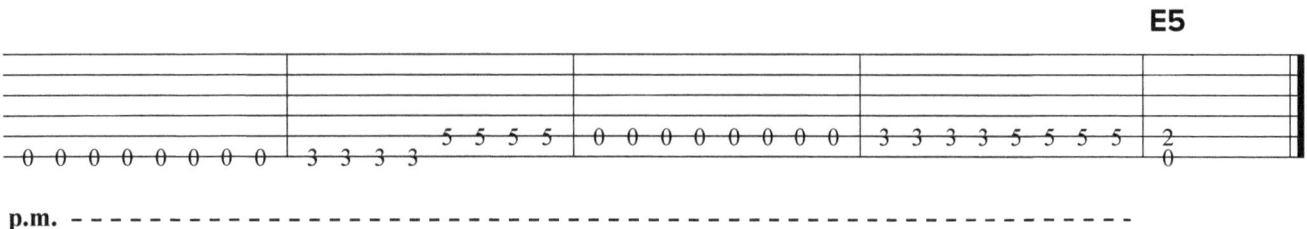

Tip:

If you'd like to learn more about chords, we recommend *Guitar Chord Master: Power Chords.* It's a 185 page guide designed to help you unlock the raw energy of power chords. Learn all the different types of power chords and how to play them all the way up the guitar neck! Find out more at TheMissingMethod.com.

Unit 7: Basics of Popular Style

- Rock
- Blues
- Jazz
- Folk
- Country
- Classical

Folk

There is no better way of learning the basics of guitar than by learning to play **folk** music. It is usually defined as old, traditional music whose composers have long since died or have been forgotten. Like folk tales, these songs have been passed down through the generations aurally (being heard and repeated), and as a result there are many variations of them.

Features of folk music include easy chord progressions; simple strumming patterns; and catchy, well-known melodies.

Since the song example below contains both notation and TAB to show you how to play the melody, it gives you no specific instructions on how to strum the song. A great deal of sheet music does this. Therefore, you get to create your own strumming patterns that you think helps support the melody. A basic strum pattern is provided on the next page to give you a place to start from.

Famous Folk

Famous Folk
(Strummed Version)

Tip: The N.C. at the beginning of this song stands for No Chord, meaning that you don't start strumming until measure 2.

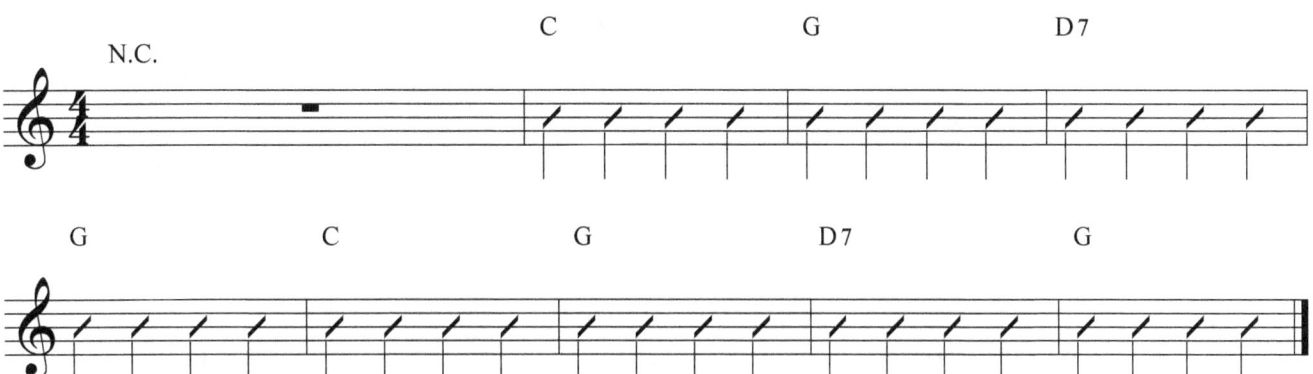

Good Night Ladies

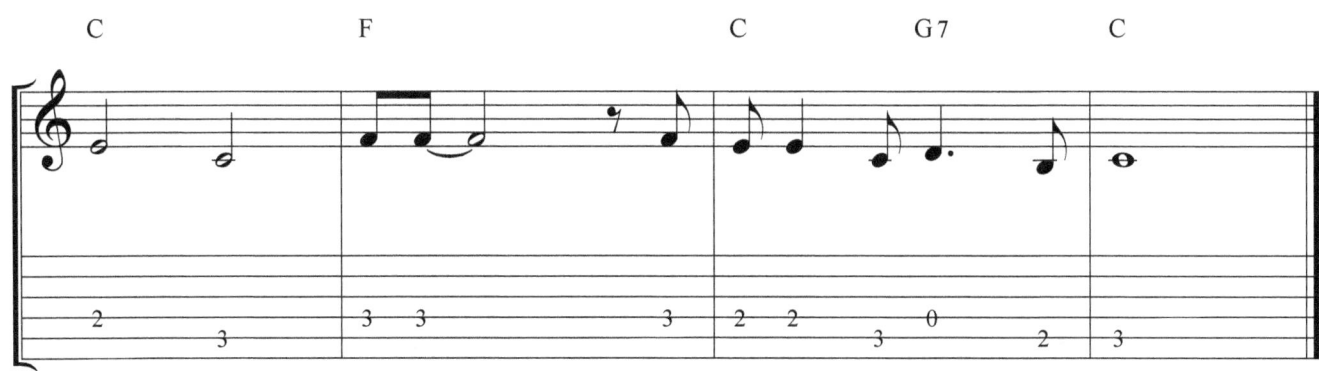

The Blues

The blues is a type of folk music and is the grandfather of all popular music from jazz, to rock, to hip-hop. Its easy-to-remember chord progression has made it a fun and ever expanding form that countless musicians use to jam along with. It started in the American Deep South among African-Americans in the late 1800s, and it quickly spread. Much of the early blues was based on folk tunes, spirituals, and call-and-response work songs. Like all the styles presented in this book, there are many different types of blues, but they all are based on similar chord progressions and melodic content.

On the next two pages are three different approaches to the blues. First, is a melody that includes blue notes, which are notes added to the major scale that give the blues its distinct sound. Second, is a typical 12-Bar Blues chord progression. Third, is a common blues riff.

Blues Melody

The 12 Bar Blues

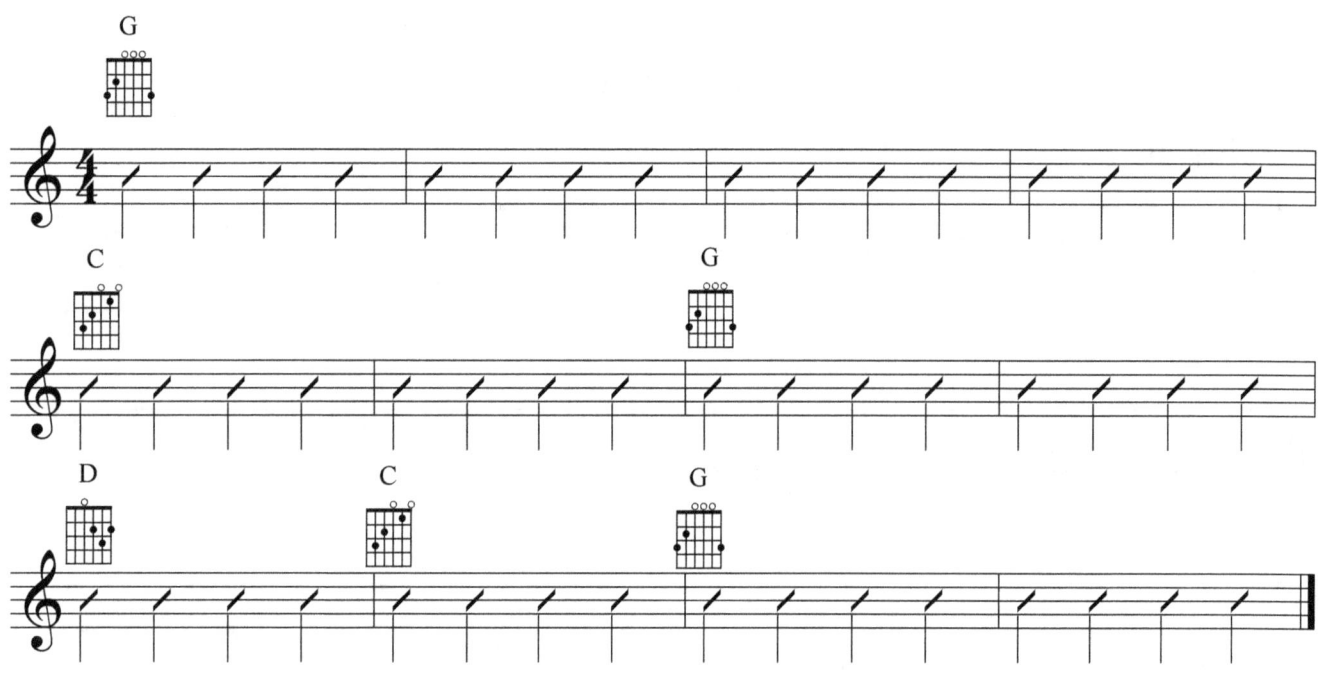

The Blues Riff

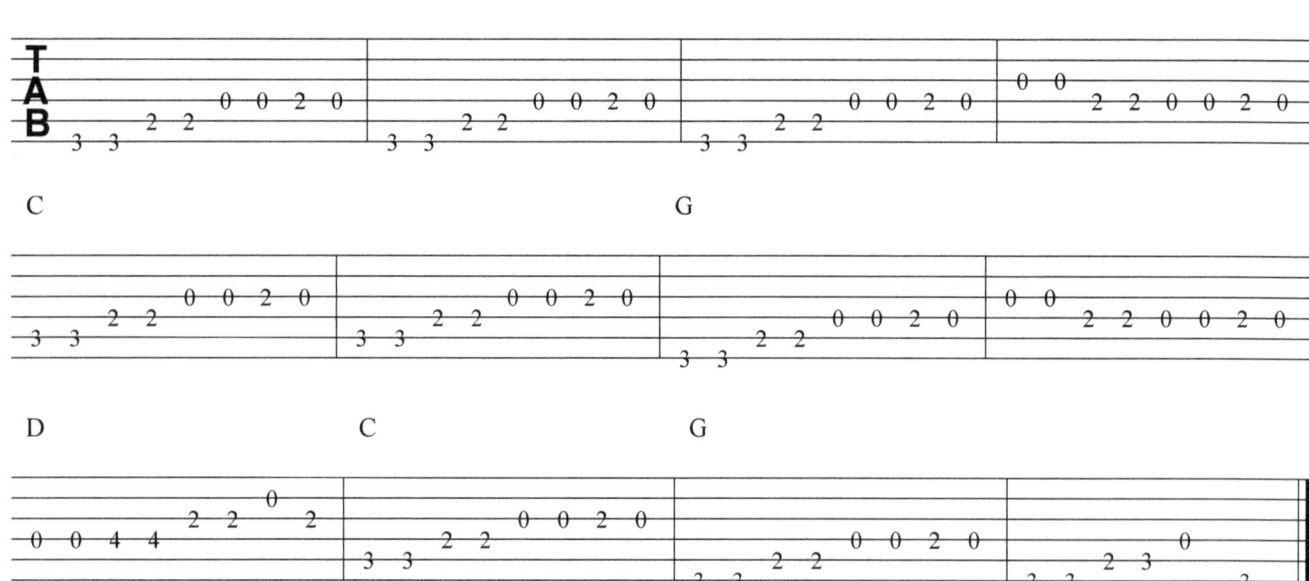

Rock

Rock music is a general term that encompasses a wide variety of styles, genres, and sub-genres. That being said, it would take an entire book to cover them all. So here, we are breaking down the basic elements of rock that are fairly universal to give you just a taste of rock n' roll.

The first element we'll talk about is the **rhythm guitar** parts. Here it is the job of the guitar player to provide a driving background. This can be done one of two main ways: **riffs** (a repeated accompaniment pattern), and **power chords** (covered in Unit 6). Below you will find an example of each.

Example Riff

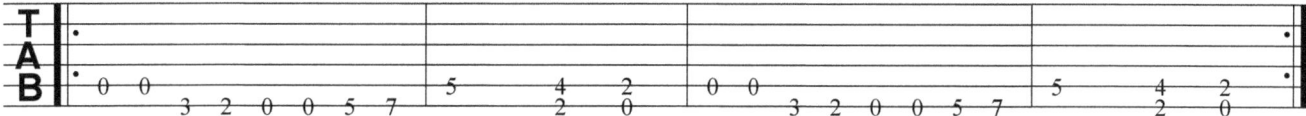

A Common Early Rock Riff

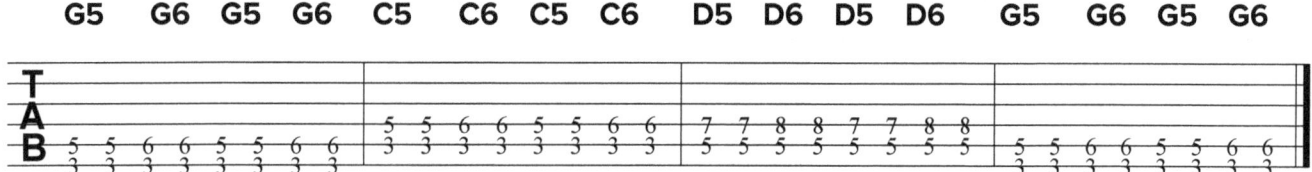

Power Chord Song Example

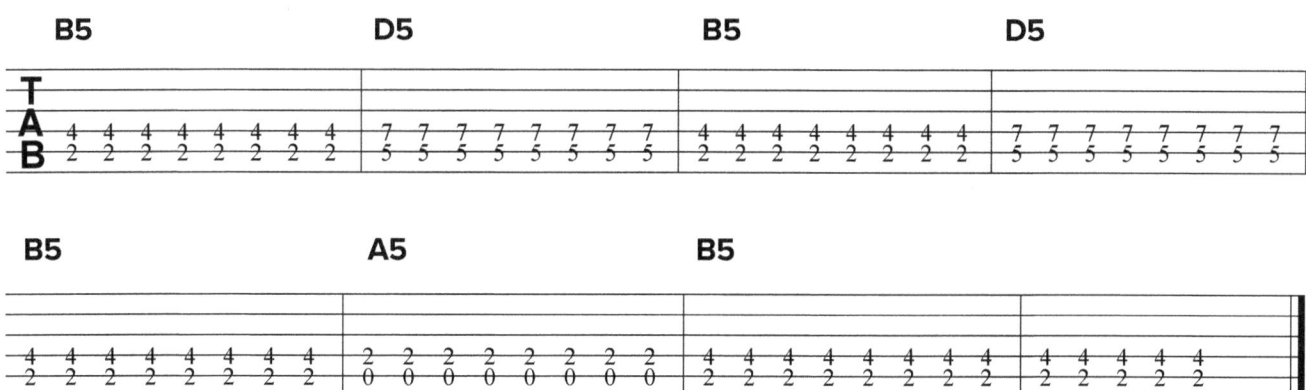

The second element is the **lead** part, which uses scale notes, often from the **pentatonic scale** (a five note scale), to cut through the background to create accents, solos, and other melodic ideas that drive the song forward. This is often where the guitar player is given the opportunity show off their chops. They often utilize articulation and effects unique to the guitar, such as string bends, vibrato, and whammy bar dives.

Minor Pentatonic Scale

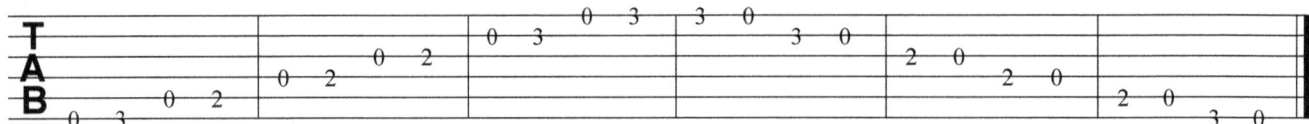

Guitar Solo Example
(Based on the Minor Pentatonic Scale)

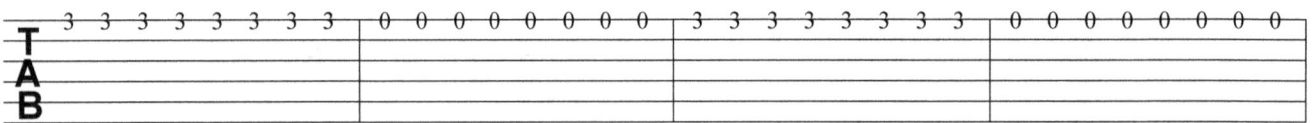

Tip:

The pentatonic scale is among the most important scales for guitar players to learn. The best way to learn it well is to incorporate into your daily warm-ups. *Technique Master, Vol 2: Pentatonic Master* can help you do just that! Visit TheMissingMethod.com to learn more.

Country

Like rock music, **country music** is a fairly general term used to cover a wide variety of music. Much of it grew out of Appalachian and other folk music (including western music and the blues) somewhere in the late 1920's. Today, it is one of the most popular, if not *the* most popular, type of music in the United States, though some would argue that modern country has just as much in common with rock as it has with older forms of country music.

When it comes to playing country music, like rock, it can be broken down into two primary approaches: lead and rhythm. However, country tends to utilize more open chords (also known as *cowboy chords*) and major pentatonic scales, rather than minor.

Below, we'll start with a bass-chord rhythm pattern in the style of Hank Williams Sr. Here, you begin by playing a single note (the bass note) followed by a chord strum.

Country Example

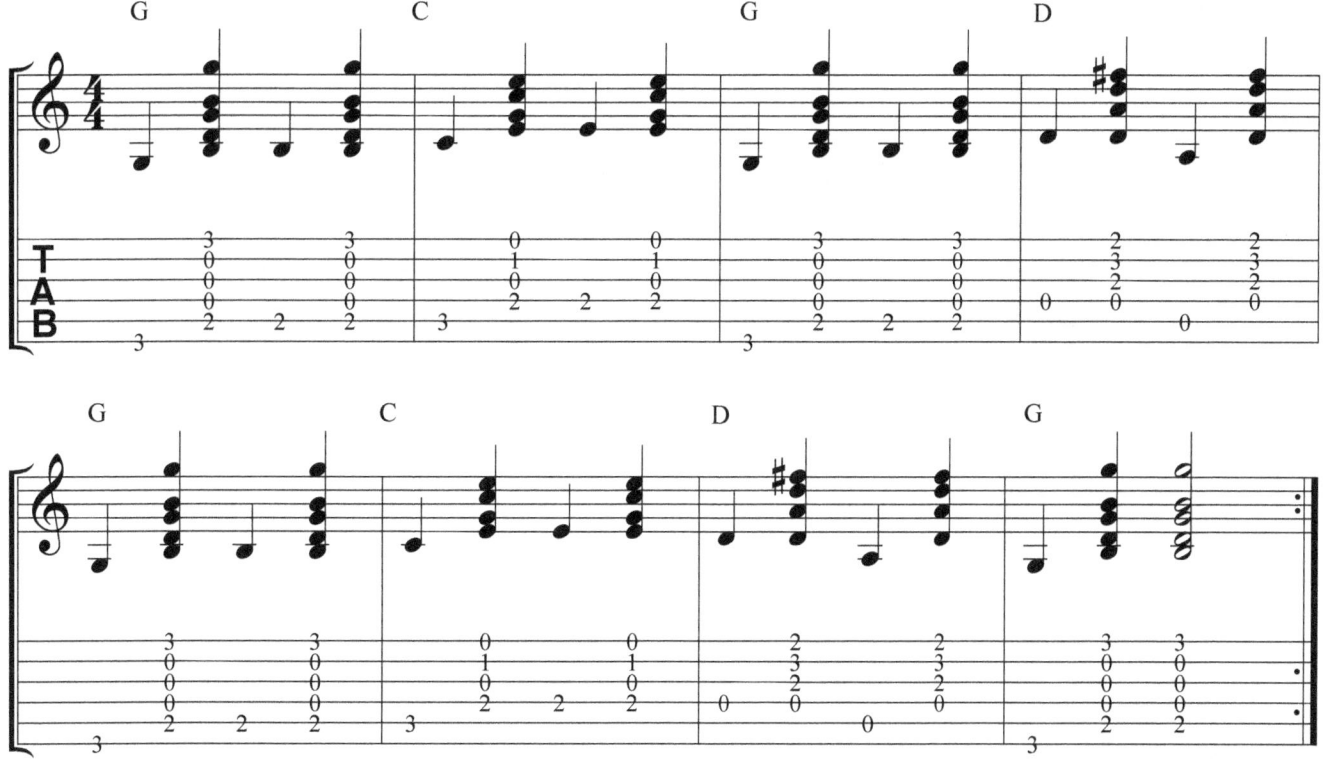

Next, we'll review Travis picking, which is a fingerstyle accompaniment used mainly in country music. (See Unit 5 for more on Travis picking.)

Travis Picking Example

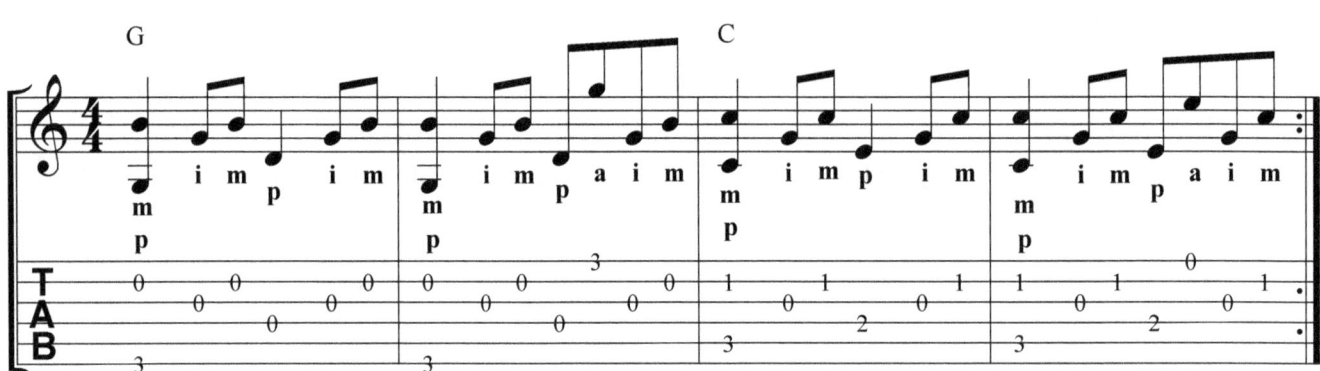

Finally, we'll take a look at the major pentatonic scale, and how it might be used in a country song.

Major Pentatonic Scale

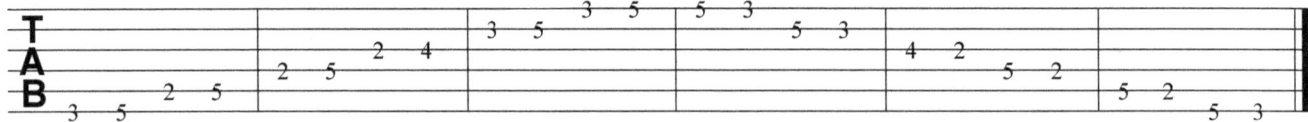

Country Lead Part

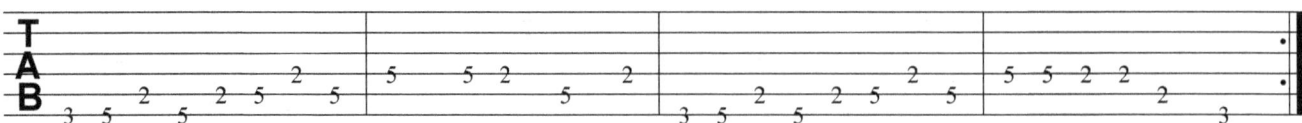

Jazz

Jazz can best be described as freedom in music, and yet it follows certain rules and structures. But from within those rules, musicians are free to fully express themselves. It started in New Orleans during the late 19th century and early 20th century and over time has transformed and been fused with all sorts of music from swing, to Be-bop, to cool, to fusion, to classic jazz standards from The Great American Songbook.

One of the main features of jazz is **improvisation**, where musicians are given a set of chords and asked to make up something on the spot. Of course, lots of practice and planning go into improvisation, but in its purest form it transcends into pure aural art.

A typical jazz tune works like this: the band will play an intro leading into what is called the head, which will contain a familiar tune. Then using the same chords from the head, the band members will take turns improvising. After everyone who wants to takes a solo, the head is played once again, telling the listener that the song is coming to an end.

The guitar was popularized in jazz with the advent of the electric guitar and one of its great early players: Charlie Christian. Before Charlie Christian, the guitar, if there was one in a jazz band, was strictly part of the rhythm section. As a result, the guitar to this day is often used to back up a soloist or band. However, Christian was among the first guitarists to improvise a solo on the guitar, and ever since, guitar players have been working hard to keep that tradition alive.

There are many, many approaches to jazz accompaniment, so here we are going to give you a basic jazz chord progression to try out.

Jazz Rhythm Example

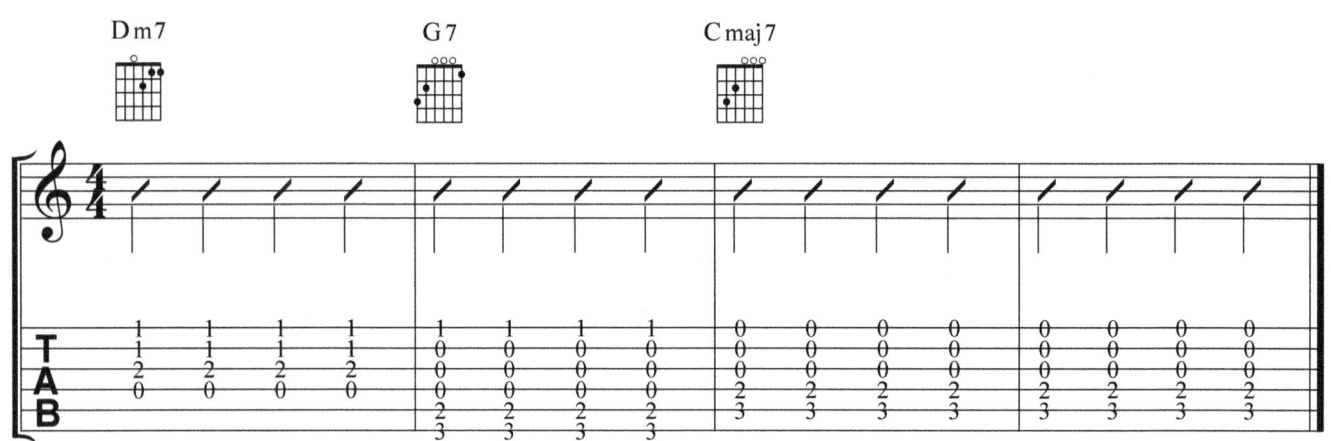

Example Jazz Tune

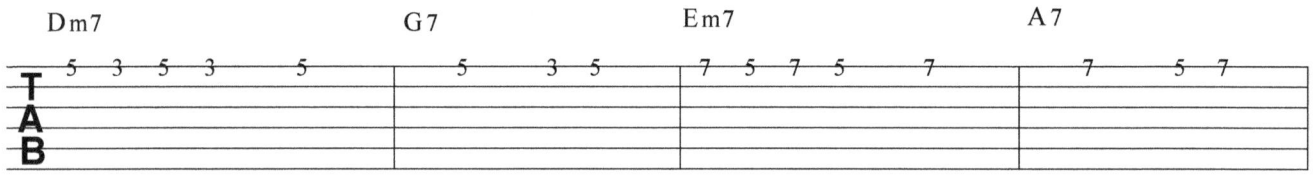

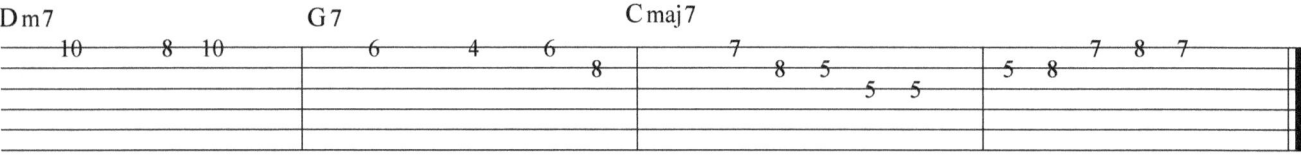

Next, you'll find the basic major scale. This scale contains all the notes that you could use to improvise while someone else plays chords.

The C Major Scale

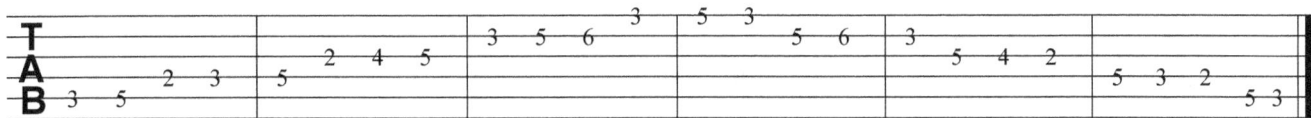

Below is an example of a possible jazz solo based on the major scale.

Example Improvised Jazz Solo

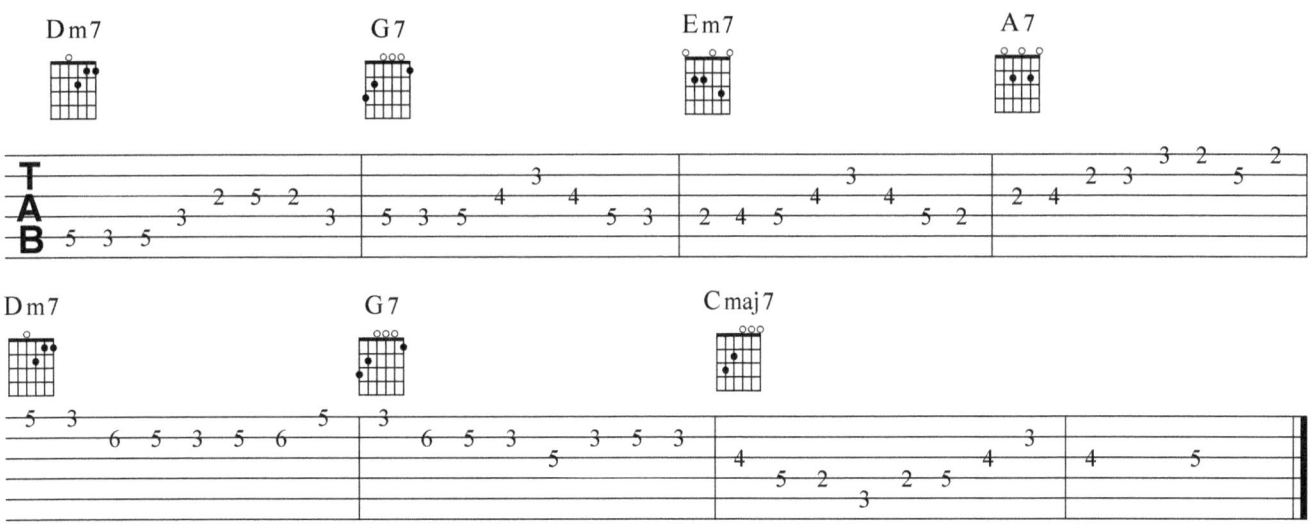

Classical

Classical music written for the guitar began during the Italian Renaissance. Though the instrument itself is thought to be older than that (possibly originating in some form in Babylon), it was during the Renaissance that we first see music written for this instrument. However, much of the repertoire from that time period actually comes from lute music. Later, during the Romantic Era of music (c.1780-1910), the guitar as we know it came into being, and a great deal of music was written for it. However, since it was a quiet instrument when compared to a trumpet or violin, it was rarely featured as an orchestral instrument, often only being used in small ensembles or as a solo instrument.

The guitar used to play classical music is different from a regular steel-string acoustic. It has a wider neck, meaning the strings are further apart to accommodate fingerpicking; the strings themselves are made of nylon, which aids in the overall tone as well as being easier on your fingers; and they deliver a rich, warm tone that can't be replicated on any other instrument. (See photo in Unit 1, Types of Guitars.)

It is possible, of course, to play music intended for the classical guitar on any type of guitar. Below are a few examples of the classical guitar approach. You should note that it is almost never played with a pick. See Unit 5, Fingerstyle before trying these out.

Renaissance Example
Tanz by Georg Fuhramnn

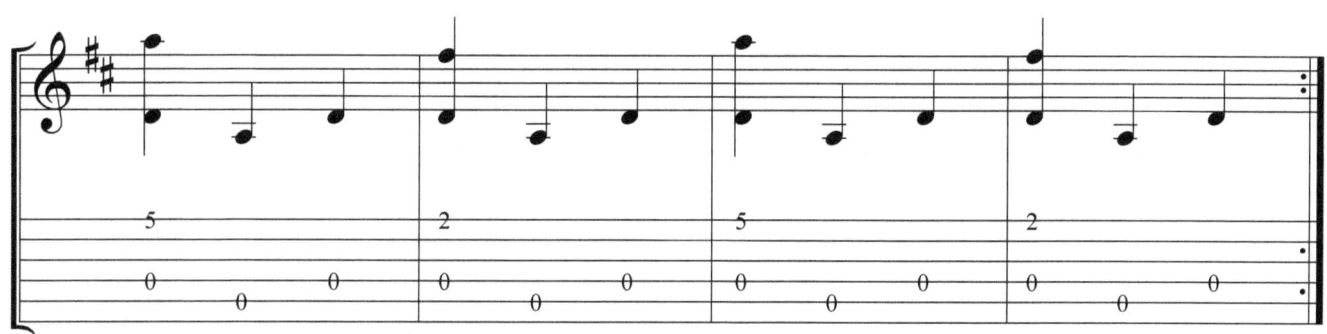

Baroque Example
Bourree by J. S. Bach

Classical Example
Andantino by M. Giuliani

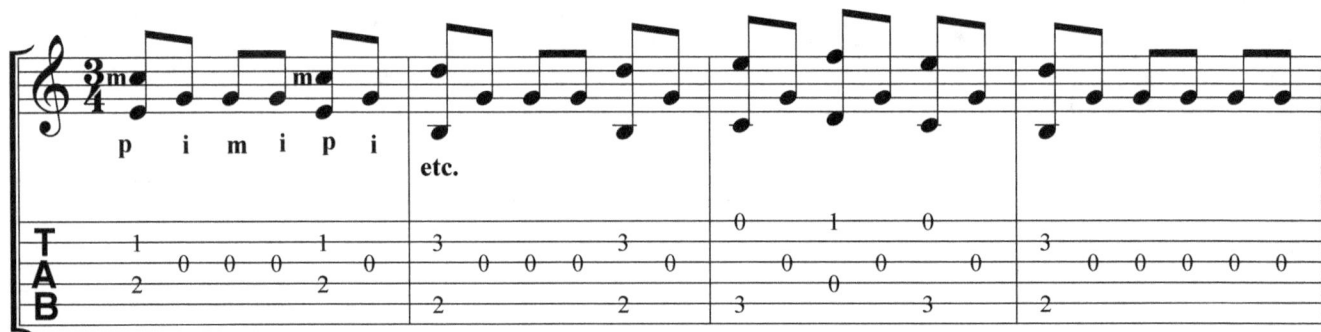

Unit 8: Ear Training

- Intervals
- Chords
- Chord Progressions
- Rhythm Training

Ear Training

Playing by ear can be difficult at first, but is an important skill to develop over time. The basic idea is that you learn what familiar patterns sound like and then learn to identify those common patterns in music you like.

Learning to play by ear is like learning a foreign language. When you hear a language you aren't familiar with, it sounds like gibberish. However, once you learn a few words in that language, you can start picking out the familiar. Music works in the same manner. Once you start learning what different chords and intervals sound like, you start hearing them in everyday songs.

Getting started playing by ear

The first thing you'll want to understand is that when you learn to play by ear, you aren't necessarily trying to develop perfect pitch, meaning that you hear a note and can tell someone what note it is. Though this can be useful, it isn't necessary. Instead, what you'll want to focus on is **relative pitch**, meaning that you can identify the relationship between sounds in order to figure out what is being played. To do this, you'll want to break down the different sounds into these categories:

- **Intervals:** the distances between notes
- **Chords and Chord Progressions:** what notes sound like when played together and in a sequence
- **Rhythm:** when a note or chord is happening in time
- **Timbre**: (pronounced tam-ber) this simply asks you to identify what instrument is playing or what effects, wood type, guitar type, etc, someone is playing. Of the list, this is the least important, but still a useful skill to have.

Intervals

Chances are you are already somewhat aware of certain intervals. An example would be a half-step, which is the smallest distance in sound between two notes. Below is a chart listing the names of the most common intervals that you'll want to learn. To learn them, play these notes on your instrument in order and listen to the sound they make. Next, try to attach that sound to a song you're familiar with that contains that exact interval. This will help you to recognize the sound much more quickly. Third, sing the interval. Even if you aren't a very good singer, it helps you to solidify the sound of each interval in your ear.

Interval Names

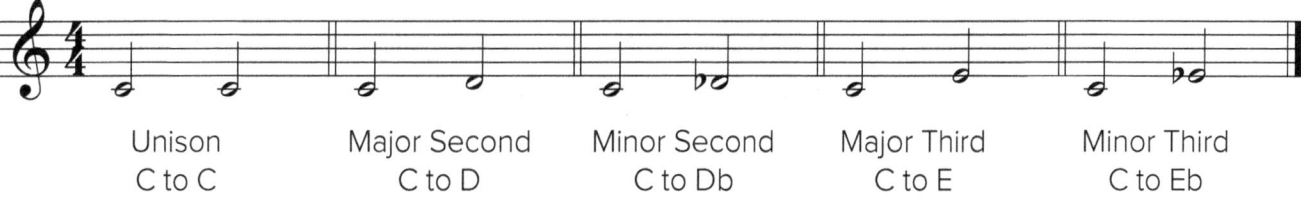

Unison
C to C

Major Second
C to D

Minor Second
C to Db

Major Third
C to E

Minor Third
C to Eb

Perfect Fourth
C to F

Augmented Fourth
or Tritone
C to F#

Perfect Fifth
C to G

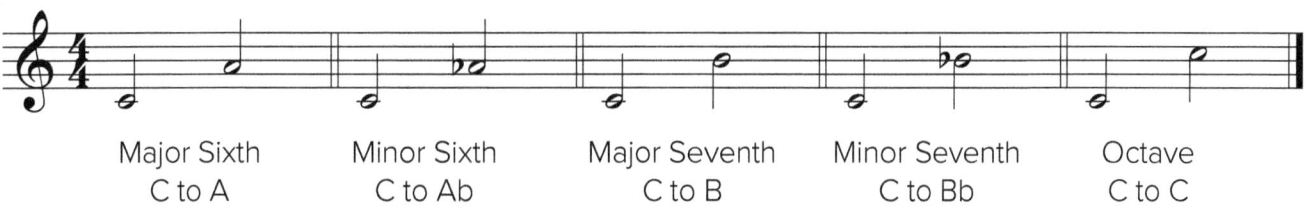

Major Sixth
C to A

Minor Sixth
C to Ab

Major Seventh
C to B

Minor Seventh
C to Bb

Octave
C to C

Interval Practice

To learn these intervals, practice them in the suggested groups below. Take your time with them, and only move on once you are fairly confident you have a set learned. Then download an ear training app to test yourself, or find an ear training partner to work with.

Set 1: Unison and Ascending Octave

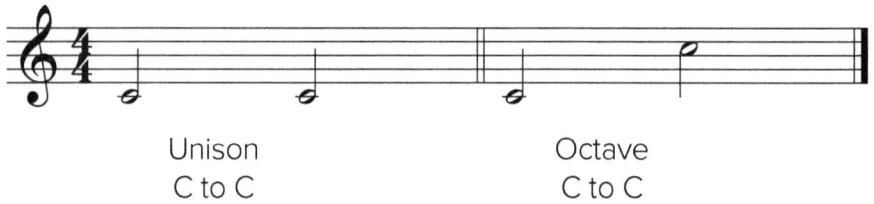

Unison
C to C

Octave
C to C

Unison is the easiest interval to learn since it's the same note. The **octave** is the next easiest. A song that may help you remember the sound of the ascending octave is *Somewhere Over the Rainbow.*

Set 2: Unison and Descending Octave

Unison
C to C

Octave
C to C

A song that may help you remember the sound of the descending octave is the jazz classic *Willow Weep for Me.*

This next set contains what are known as **perfect intervals**. They are called this because they don't have a major or minor version. For the **perfect fourth**, the song *Here Comes the Bride* is often suggested. For the **perfect fifth**, the opening notes to the theme from *Star Wars* works well.

Set 3: Ascending Perfect Fourth and Perfect Fifth

Perfect Fourth
C to F

Perfect Fifth
C to G

Set four contains the same intervals as set 3, however, this time they are descending. *I've Been Working on the Railroad* works for the perfect fourth, and *The Flintstones* opening notes works for the perfect fifth.

Set 4: Descending Perfect Fourth and Perfect Fifth

Perfect Fourth
F to C

Perfect Fifth
G to C

Set 5: Ascending Major Third and Minor Third

Major Third
C to E

Minor Third
C to Eb

Set 5 contains the intervals that make up the basis for most chords: the third. Here, like the seconds, we have **major third** and **minor third**. The song *Michael Row Your Boat Ashore* can help you to remember the major third and the folk song *Greensleeves* or the Christmas song *What Child is This?* works for the minor third.

Set 6: Descending Major Third and Minor Third

Major Third
E to C

Minor Third
Eb to C

A song that may help you remember the sound of the descending major third is the jazz classic *Summertime*. For the minor third, think of *Hey Jude*.

Set 7: Ascending Major Second and Minor Second

For the **major second**, think *Rudolf the Red-Nose Reindeer.* For the **minor second** the *Theme from Jaws* works well.

Set 8: Descending Major Second and Minor Second

For the major second use the song *Mary Had a Little Lamb* and for the minor second, *Joy to the World.*

Set 9: Review of Seconds and Thirds

Set 10: The Tritone and a Review of Perfect Intervals

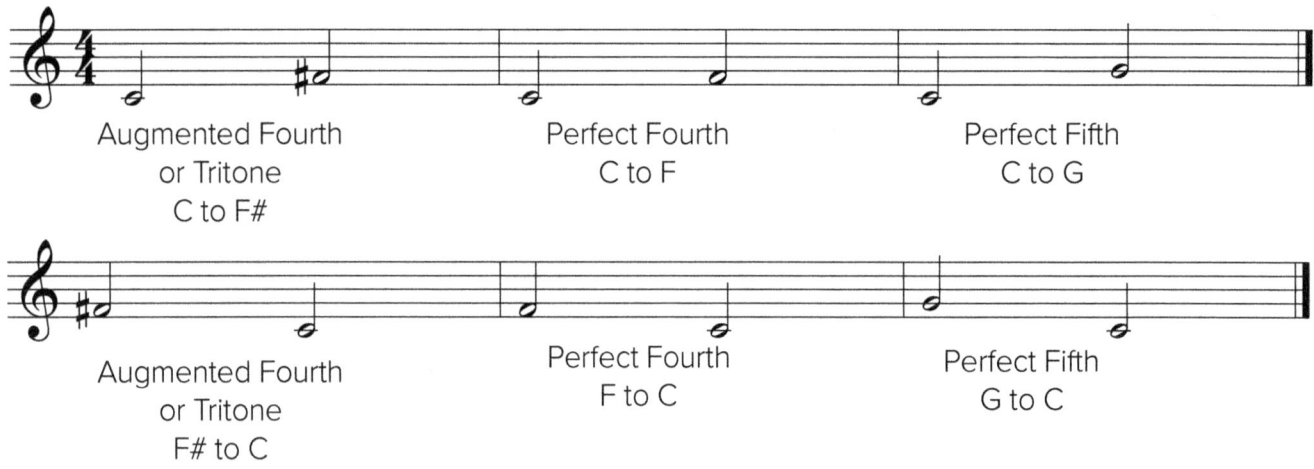

The term **tritone** (the interval of an **augmented fourth**) comes from the fact that it is three whole steps from its starting point. This interval used to be considered so dissonant that it was called the devil in music. However, it is widely used in a variety of music usually to add interest or tension. An example song using the tritone is the opening notes of the theme to the TV show *The Simpsons*.

Set 11: Ascending Major and Minor Sixth

Major Sixth
C to A

Minor Sixth
C to Ab

For the **major sixth** use the old folk song *My Bonnie* and for the **minor sixth** think of the Scott Joplin tune *The Entertainer*.

Set 12: Descending Major and Minor Sixth

Major Sixth
A to C

Minor Sixth
Ab to C

For the major sixth refer to the song *Nobody Knows the Trouble I've Seen*, and for the minor sixth *Love Story*.

Set 13: Ascending Major and Minor Seventh

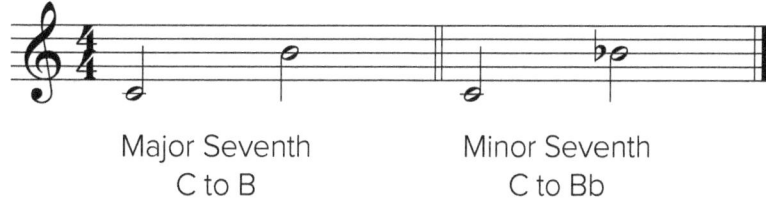

Major Seventh
C to B

Minor Seventh
C to Bb

For the **major seventh** listen to *The Immigrant Song* by Led Zeppelin, and for the **minor seventh** *The Original Star Trek Theme*.

Set 14: Descending Major and Minor Seventh

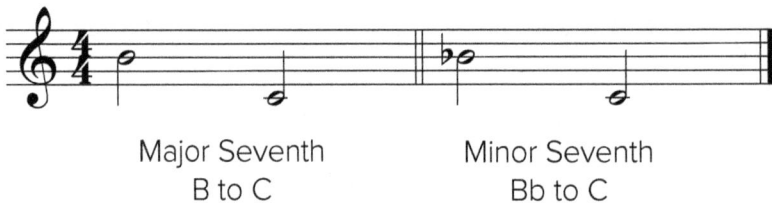

Here's where it gets a litter harder to find songs that use these intervals at the start of the song. Here's some suggestions: for the descending major seventh listen to the song *I Love You* by Cole Porter and for the minor seventh, *Watermelon Man* by Herbie Hancock.

Set 15: Reviewing Sixths and Sevenths

Chords and Chord Progressions

Chords are typically built in thirds, meaning that each note of a chord is three notes away from each other. In a major chord there are three notes: the root, the third, and the fifth. Using C as an example, it contains the notes C, E, and G. C to E is a **major third** and E to G is a **minor third**. This combination of thirds will always result in a major chord. Therefore, a major third plus a minor third equals a major chord. A minor chord is the other way around: a minor third plus a major third. These two sounds make up a great deal of music and is the first thing you'll want to be able to recognize quickly. Major is typically described as "bright" or "happy," and minor is lower or "sad" sounding.

To practice these, simply listen to a major chord then a minor chord to hear the differences. Most ear training apps will include these features.

Thirds Example

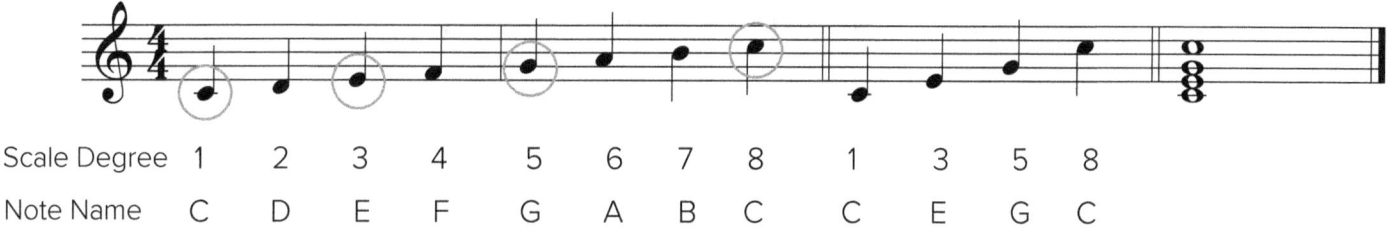

Note: Even though the G to the last C is not a third, the note C is already in the chord, therefore it is usually included to round out the sound.

The Major Chord

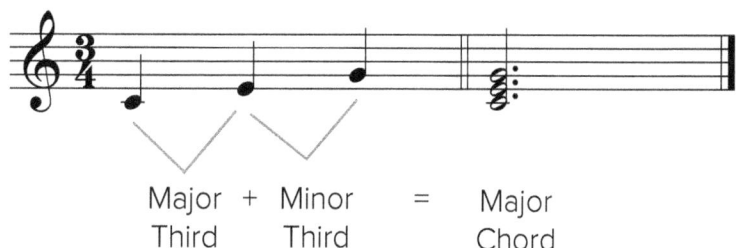

The Minor Chord

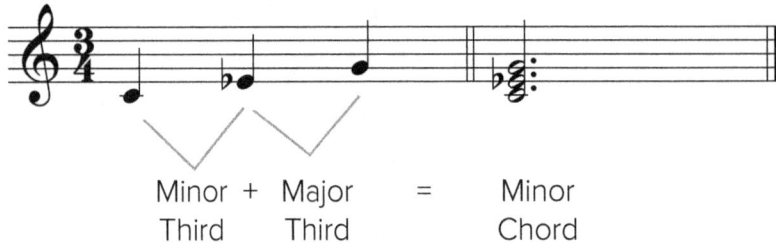

Once you can clearly hear the difference between major and minor, your next step is to listen to dominant sevenths and major sevenths. A dominant seventh chord is made up of a major chord, plus another minor third on top. A major seventh is made up of a major chord plus a major third on top.

The Dominant Seventh Chord

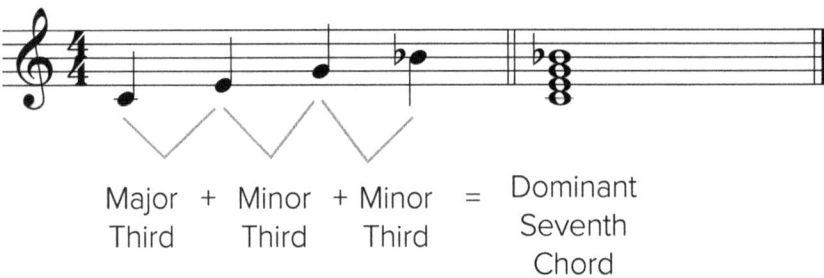

The Major Seventh Chord

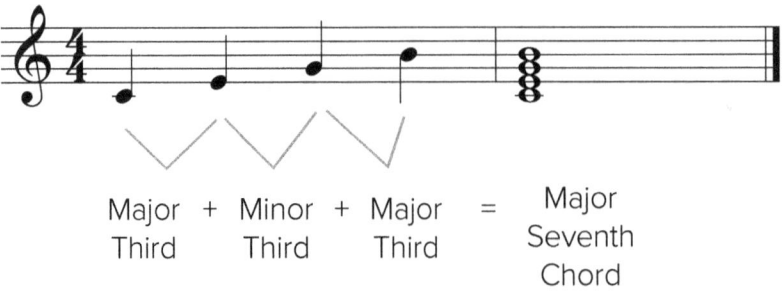

Practice 1: Listen to the Major Chord

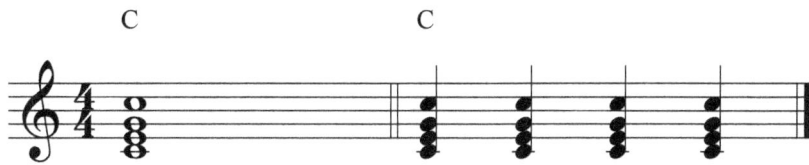

Practice 2: Listen to the Minor Chord

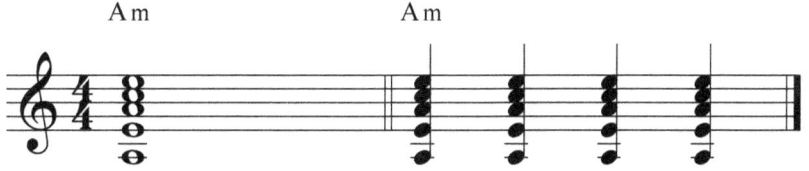

Practice 3: Listen to the Dominant Seventh Chord

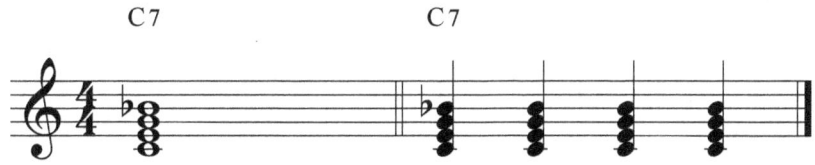

Practice 4: Listen to the Major Seventh Chord

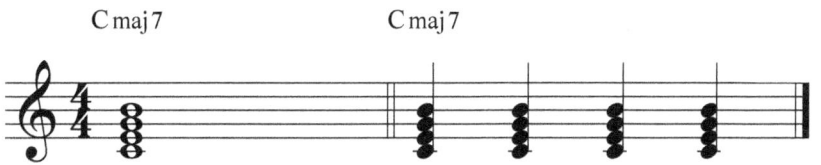

Practice 5: Listen to each type of chord to hear the differences

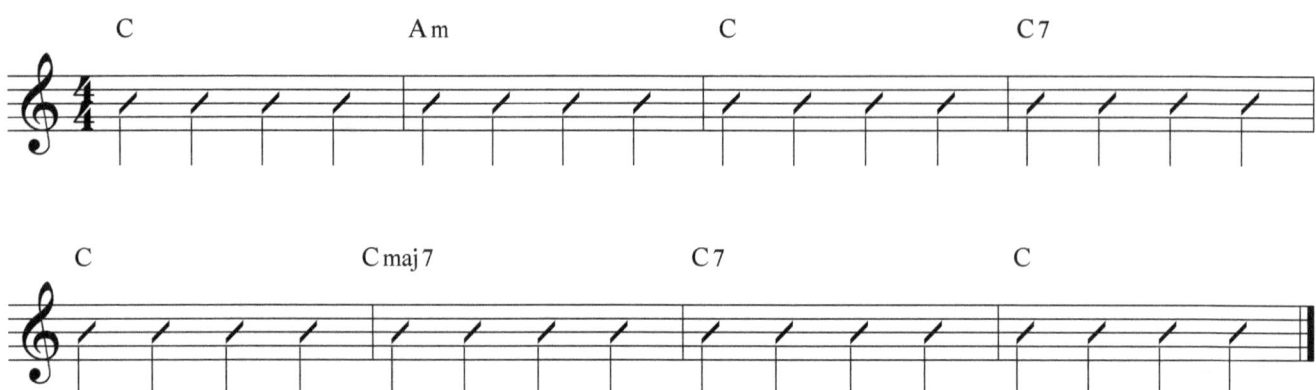

Chord Progressions

After you are familiar with these sounds, your next step is listen for chords in a series, also called a **chord progression.** There are two common chord progressions that you should start with.

First is a chord progression called the IV (4), V (5), I (1). These numbers refer to where the roots of these chords fall in the major scale. Therefore in the key of G, these chords would be: C (IV), D (V), and G (I). Strumming these chords in this sequence will help you to recognize this pattern. It may even sound familiar to you when you first play it.

Practice 1: Listen to the following Chord Progression

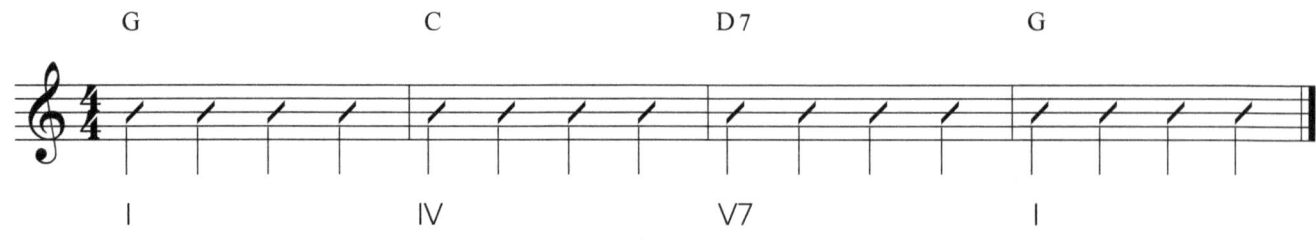

The second common chord progression is called the **turnaround** chord progression. It is called this because it sounds like its turning the sound back around, taking you back to the beginning.

There are several different turnarounds in music, but here we will try out the most common one: (I) (vi) (IV) (V), or in the key of G: G, Em, C, D7. When you play this progression, you will notice that it sounds like it wants to continue back to the G chord. So to end it, simply play the G chord.

Practice 2: Listen to the following Chord Progression

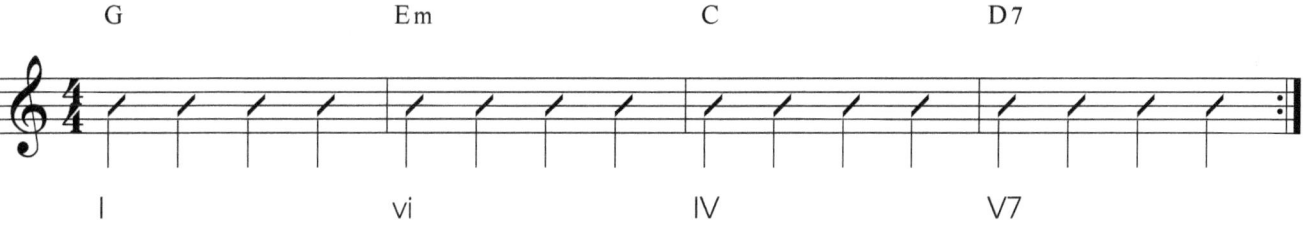

Finally, listen to the blues and see how many of these chord progressions you can identify. You can also listen to great deal of popular music and hear examples of these chord progressions.

Practice 3: Listen to the following Chord Progression

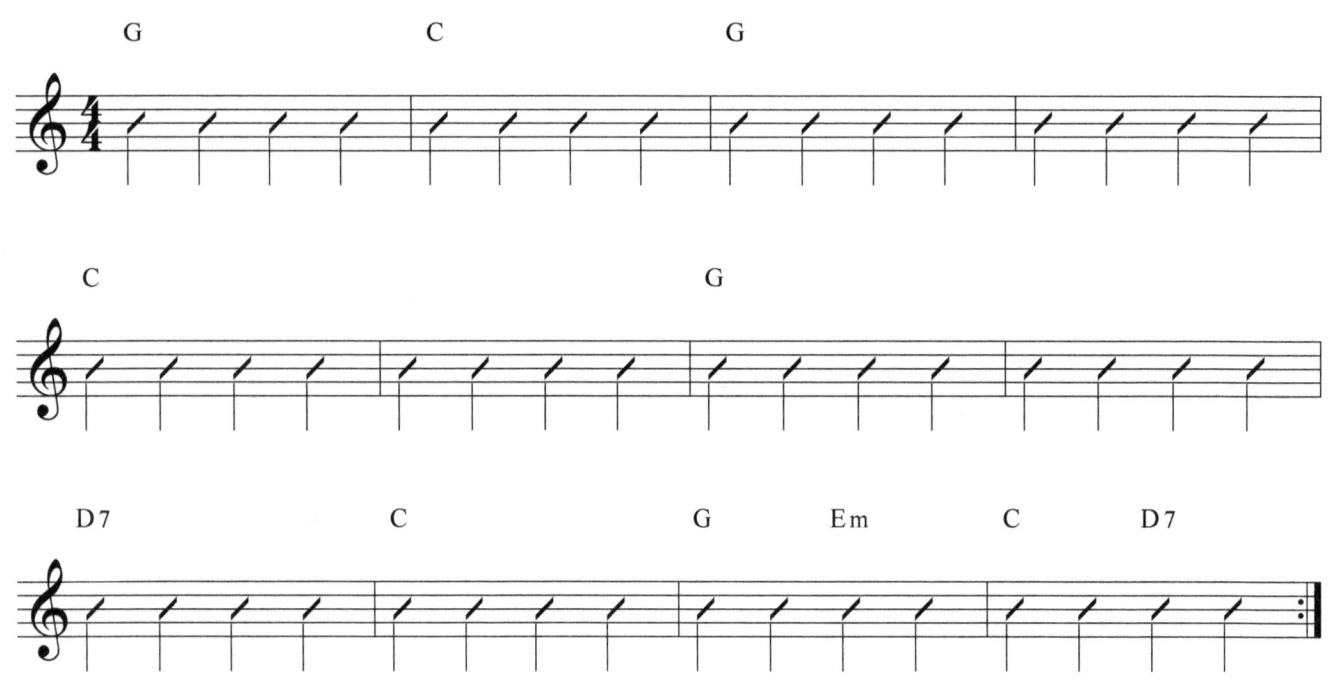

Take the time to listen to each chord progression carefully as you play them. Also, be sure to practice these as often as possible, a minimum of once a day until your ear grows used to the sounds.

Rhythm Training

Though listening and understanding the basic sounds of music is a fantastic foundation from which to build, you also need to be able to figure out rhythms. **Rhythm** is only one element of time in music. **Beat** is the underlying heartbeat of any piece of music, and rhythm is what you are actually playing, or how long or how short each note is being played.

Step 1:

The first step in being able to figure out the rhythm is to figure out the **meter**, or how the beats are grouped together. Most of the time, this will be in groups of four called four-four time. Beats can also be grouped in threes (three-four time). There are plenty of other possible groupings, but these are much rarer and can often be boiled down to groups of two, three, four, or some combination of them.

Example 1: Groups of Four

Example 2: Groups of Three

Step 2:

Feel the beat. This is accomplished by figuring out the tempo, or how fast or slow the song is being played, and then determining the meter. Once you know that, start counting along with the beat. (Ex: 1, 2, 3, 4).

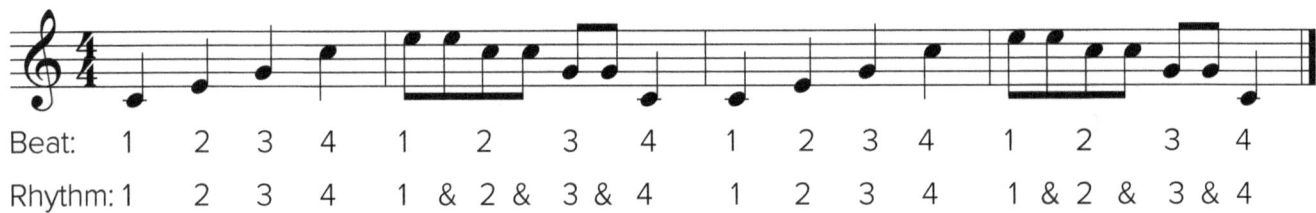

Step 3:

Start to figure out how many notes are being played per beat. This will help you figure out if they have divided the beat into **quarter notes** (one note per beat), **eighth notes** (two notes per beat), **triplets** (three notes per beat), or **sixteenth notes** (four notes per beat). These are not the only possibilities, but these are by far the most common and the easiest to figure out. Don't worry if you can't figure out a difficult rhythm, this is only the beginning of your rhythm training. Keep things as easy, understandable, and simple for yourself as possible. But also be sure to challenge yourself.

Note: the following exercises do not cover every possible rhythm, but should give you a strong foundation from which to begin.

Example 1: Quarter Notes

Example 2: Eighth Notes

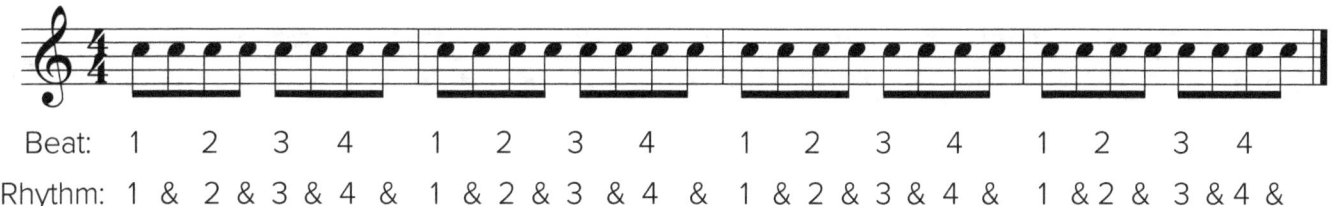

Beat: 1   2   3   4   1   2   3   4   1   2   3   4   1   2   3   4
Rhythm: 1 & 2 & 3 & 4 &   1 & 2 & 3 & 4 &   1 & 2 & 3 & 4 &   1 & 2 & 3 & 4 &

Example 3: Triplet Notes

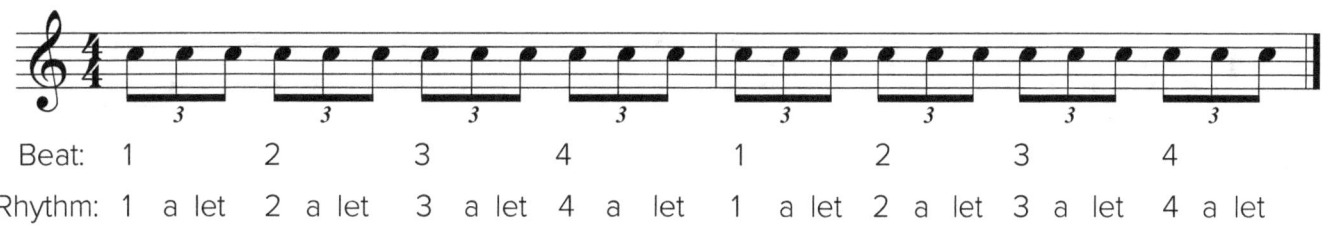

Beat: 1   2   3   4   1   2   3   4
Rhythm: 1 a let   2 a let   3 a let   4 a let   1 a let   2 a let   3 a let   4 a let

Example 4: Sixteenth Notes

Beat: 1   2   3   4   1   2   3   4
Rhythm: 1 e & a 2 e & a 3 e & a 4 e & a   1 e & a 2 e & a 3 e & a 4 e & a

Example 5: Eighths and Sixteenths

Beat: 1   2   3   4   1   2   3   4
Rhythm: 1   & a   2   & a   3   & a   4   & a   1   & a   2   & a   3   & a   4   & a

161

Example 6: Eighths and Sixteenths

Beat: 1   2   3   4   1   2   3   4

Rhythm: 1 e &   2 e &   3 e &   4 e &   1 e &   2 e &   3 e &   4 e &

Example 7: Eighths and Sixteenths

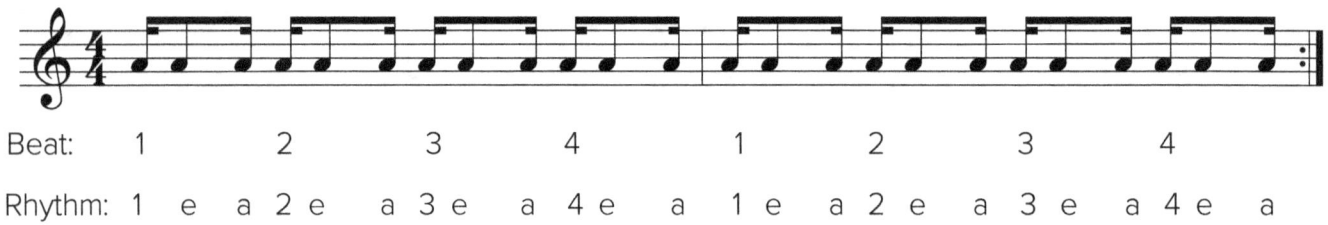

Beat: 1   2   3   4   1   2   3   4

Rhythm: 1 e   a 2 e   a 3 e   a 4 e   a 1 e   a 2 e   a 3 e   a 4 e   a

Example 8 : Dotted Quarter Notes

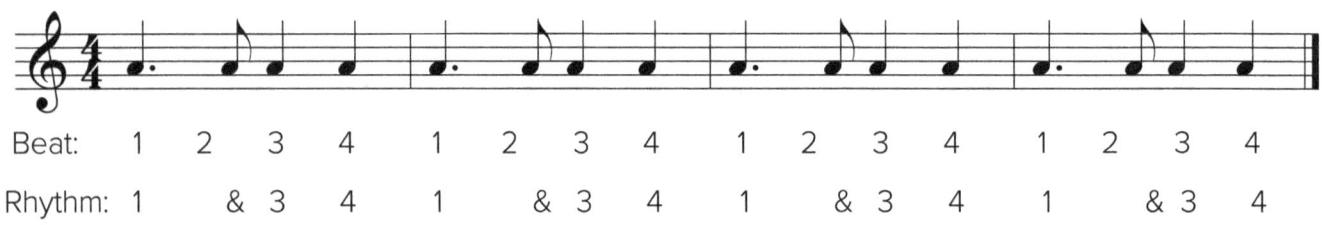

Beat: 1   2   3   4   1   2   3   4   1   2   3   4   1   2   3   4

Rhythm: 1   & 3 4   1   & 3 4   1   & 3 4   1   & 3 4

Example 9: Dotted Eighth Notes

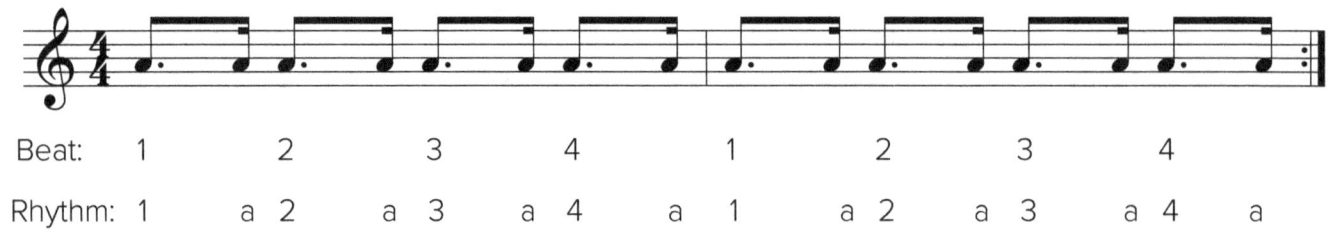

Beat: 1   2   3   4   1   2   3   4

Rhythm: 1   a 2   a 3   a 4   a 1   a 2   a 3   a 4   a

Example 10: Combining Rhythms

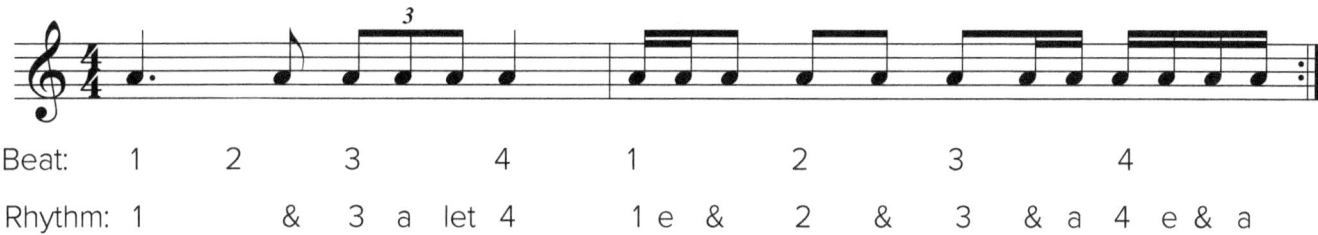

Beat:	1		2	3			4	1	e	&	2	&	3	&	a	4	e	&	a
Rhythm:	1		&	3	a	let	4	1	e	&	2	&	3	&	a	4	e	&	a

More Ear Training Tips

It's best to practice ear training every day. In addition to the exercises above, try taking easy-sounding songs and see what you can pick out of them. This can help you learn to identify the sounds and rhythms listed above. Keep in mind: you don't want this exercise to be a bunch of guesses. Listen closely to little sections and see what sounds familiar to you. If nothing does yet, don't worry. Like practicing the guitar, it takes a while for your ear to tune in and begin recognizing these familiar sounds and patterns. Keep at it, and you'll begin to see steady progress.

Appendix

- Changing Strings
- Using a Metronome
- Chord Reference Chart

How to Change Your Strings

The first time I changed my strings I had no one to show me how to do it. I also had no books or videos to refer to. It was just me, a pack of new strings, a pair of old pliers and a whole lot of frustration. That first time took me over three hours. Now, after years of practice, I can change an entire set of strings in about twenty minutes with no trouble (usually). Though every type of guitar is different, there are a few basic steps you'll want to take to make sure the string change goes smoothly.

Step 1: Though you can remove all the strings and simply replace them, this is not recommended. It is best to keep some tension on the neck at all times. Therefore, it is often recommended to change the strings in sets of two. For example: first remove strings 6 and 3, then replace them; then remove strings 5 and 2, then replace them; finally remove strings 4 and 1, then replace them. That way the tension on the neck remains fairly constant so that you won't have to make any neck adjustments after your new strings are on.

Step 2: To remove an old string, unwind the string using the tuning keys. Next, on acoustics, remove the string peg at the bridge of the guitar. You may want to use a string winding tool to assist you with both of these tasks. The other end of the winder can be used to pry the string peg free. On an electric, the string will either need to be pulled out from the back (on most Fenders, for example) or simply removed from the bridge in some way. Once this is done, return to the post on the head stock and remove the wound part of the string from around the post.

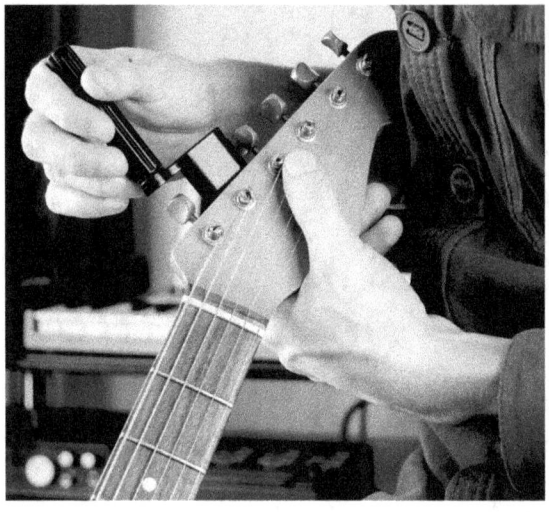

Using a string winder

Step 3: Once the old string is removed, you can then place the new string on. The first step is to place the new string in the bridge. On acoustics, place the ball end of the string into the peg-hole, then place the peg back in its place over the string (see photo on opposite page). On electrics, place the ball end of the string as it was in the bridge before. If the string came out the back, you'll need to feed the string through the back in this step. (Note: Floyd Rose, a specialty bridge, and other string-locking systems use a different approach.)

Step 4: Once the string is firmly in place in the bridge, your next step is to attach the string by winding it around the post on the headstock. To do this, first pull the string taught. Then you'll notice that you have way too much string to work with. What I do is cut the top of the string using wire cutters. Be careful not to cut too much, otherwise you'll need to get a new set of strings and start over. I usually cut about two to three inches depending on which string I'm putting on and how much slack I need. Once the string is cut, feed the tip of the string through the hole in the post. Then bend the string around the post, tucking it under itself as you bend it around. Then hold your thumb over the nut to keep the string steady. This will help you wrap it around the post neatly. Use the winding tool (or your hand) to wind the string. Continue winding until it is tight. Do not over-wind. It could break the string.

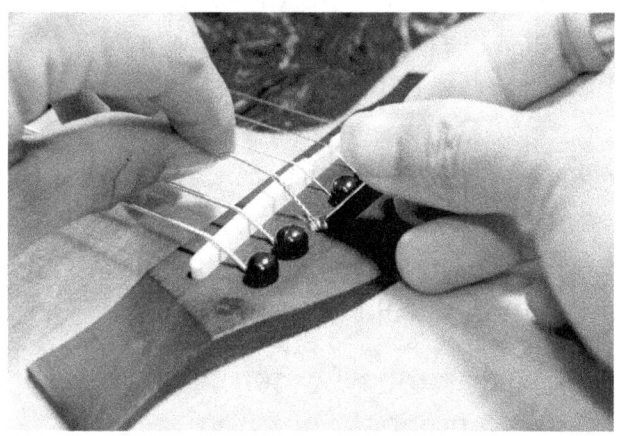

Place the ball end of the string into the peg-hole on acoustics.

Note: Make sure you take careful note as to what the strings looked like before you removed them. You'll want to make sure you don't wind the wrong way around the post.

Step 5: Once all the strings are in place, tune the guitar a half step higher than usual. This will stretch the strings and allow them to more quickly stabilize. Once all the strings are tuned high, go back and tune them to standard tuning.

Step 6: If you still have excess string hanging off the end, simply cut it off with wire cutters. Though for some scraggly wires look cool, they often end up getting in the way and can even scratch up the finish of your instrument.

How to Practice with a Metronome

When you are first starting any instrument, practicing with a metronome can seem frustrating or even impossible at times. The fact of the matter is that it is something you'll want to get good at and *can* once you know how. One obstacle can be physical movement. For some, it won't yet be possible to move fast enough to lock in with the metronome. Don't worry; with practice and time, you'll be able to use the metronome without any trouble.

There are many different types of metronomes out there, from the traditional wind-up, piano top metronome, to apps for your phone or tablet. They all work well and do about the same thing. Their purpose is to provide the beat for you (see Unit 8, Ear Training for more on *beat*).

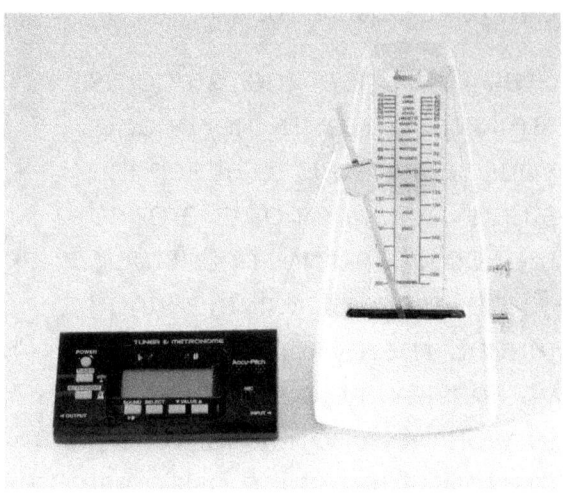

An electronic metronome (left) and traditional metronome (right).

Step One: Getting Comfortable with the Metronome

To start using the metronome, turn it on and select a relatively slow beat. I recommend somewhere around 60 beats per minute (bpm). Before you do anything, listen to the beat. Then begin by tapping your foot along with the beat. Be sure to anticipate each beat and play with the metronome. Don't wait for the click then tap your foot. Tap with it in sync.

Once you feel in sync with the metronome, begin to count out loud along with the clicks: 1, 2, 3, 4, over and over again. Keep your foot tapping while you do this. Feel the pulse; feel you footfalls; feel the time and lock in.

Stop the metronome, but keep tapping at the same rate of speed. After about 30 seconds, turn the metronome back on to see how close you've come. Chances are you will have either sped up or slowed down. That's normal. Everyone has a different heart rate, and this can affect your perception of time. But with practice, you'll start to feel different tempos and different meters.

Step Two: Practicing Your Guitar with the Metronome

Once you feel comfortable with step one, pick up your guitar and take time to get in sync with the metronome. To do this, choose any open string and play this string while you tap your foot, listen to the click, and count out loud.

Next, try it with any chord. Simply tap your foot with the metronome clicking while you strum.

After that, take any song or exercise and play only the first full phrase or measure, that way you can focus on the time more so than on the pitches. After one phrase or measure is complete, move on to the next one, repeating the process. Once you have a couple of phrases or measures down with the metronome, turn it off again and try playing just as accurately without it.

The key here is that you DON'T want to try and play an entire song with the metronome yet. Instead, use it to help you focus your practicing of small sections so you can play them more accurately.

Keep in mind that even seasoned professionals still use metronomes to practice. It's the best way to help you focus on your timing, which is crucial for playing with others, as well as sounding your best overall. Time is often overlooked by new players since the early focus is on the right notes, chords, or just getting your fingers in the right spots, but once you have all that, you have to be aware of and practice your timing.

Tip:

A great way to practice with your metronome is to try it with the exercises in the Rhythm Training section of this book. Also check out *Technique Master: 53 Warm-ups to Revolutionize Your Guitar Playing*. Each exercise is designed to be used with your metronome!

TAB Articulation Chart

Half-Step Bend: Play the note, then bend the string a half-step.

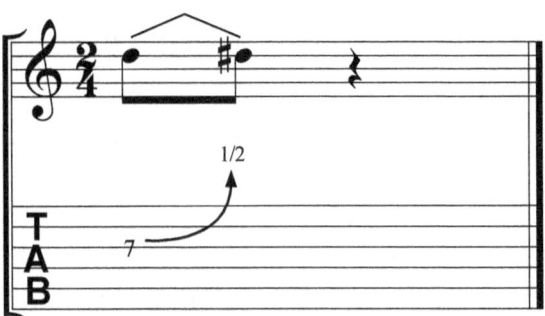

Whole-Step Bend: Play the note, then bend the string a whole-step.

Quarter-Step Bend: Play the note, then bend the string a quarter-step.

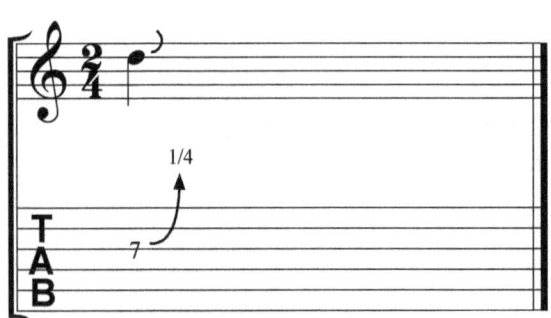

Grace Note Bend: Play the note, then bend the string right away as indicated.

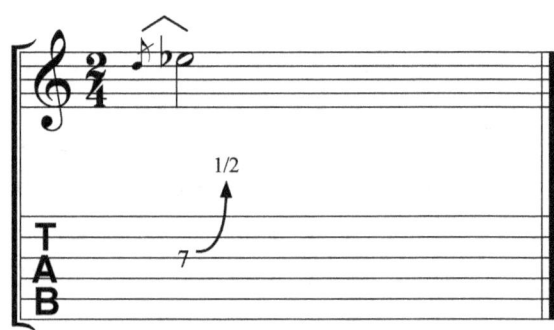

Bend and Release: Play the note, bend the string as indicated, then return to the original note.

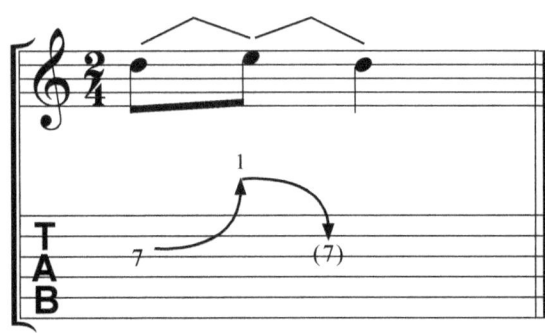

Pre-Bend: Bend to the desired pitch, then play the note.

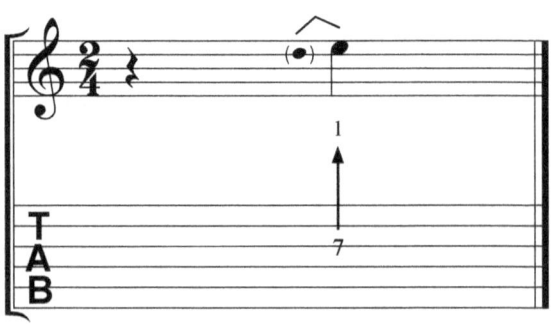

Hammer On: Play the first note with the first finger, then without picking, hammer down the third finger onto the second note so that it sounds.

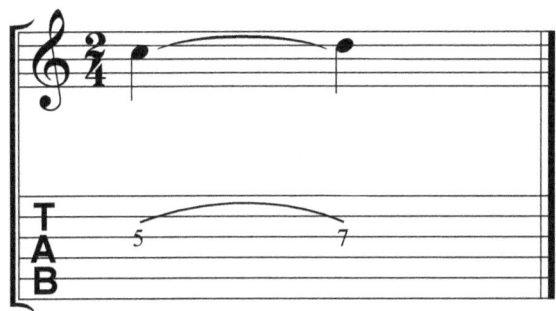

Pull Off: (Also called a **Pluck-Off**) Place both fingers down first, one on the D, one on the C, then using the finger on the note D, pull the finger off so that the note below it is heard.

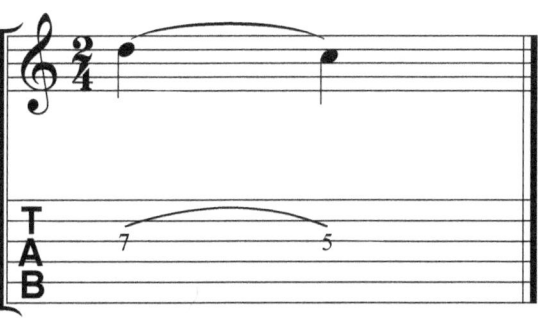

Slides: Play the first note, then without lifting your finger off, slide to the next note. (The example below is a descending slide. They can also go the other direction.)

Vibrato: Bend and release the note rapidly creating a "wave-like" sound effect.

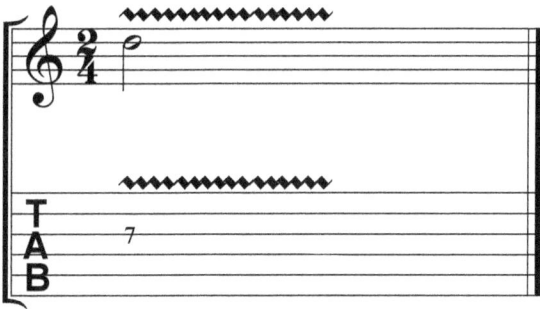

Chord Reference Chart

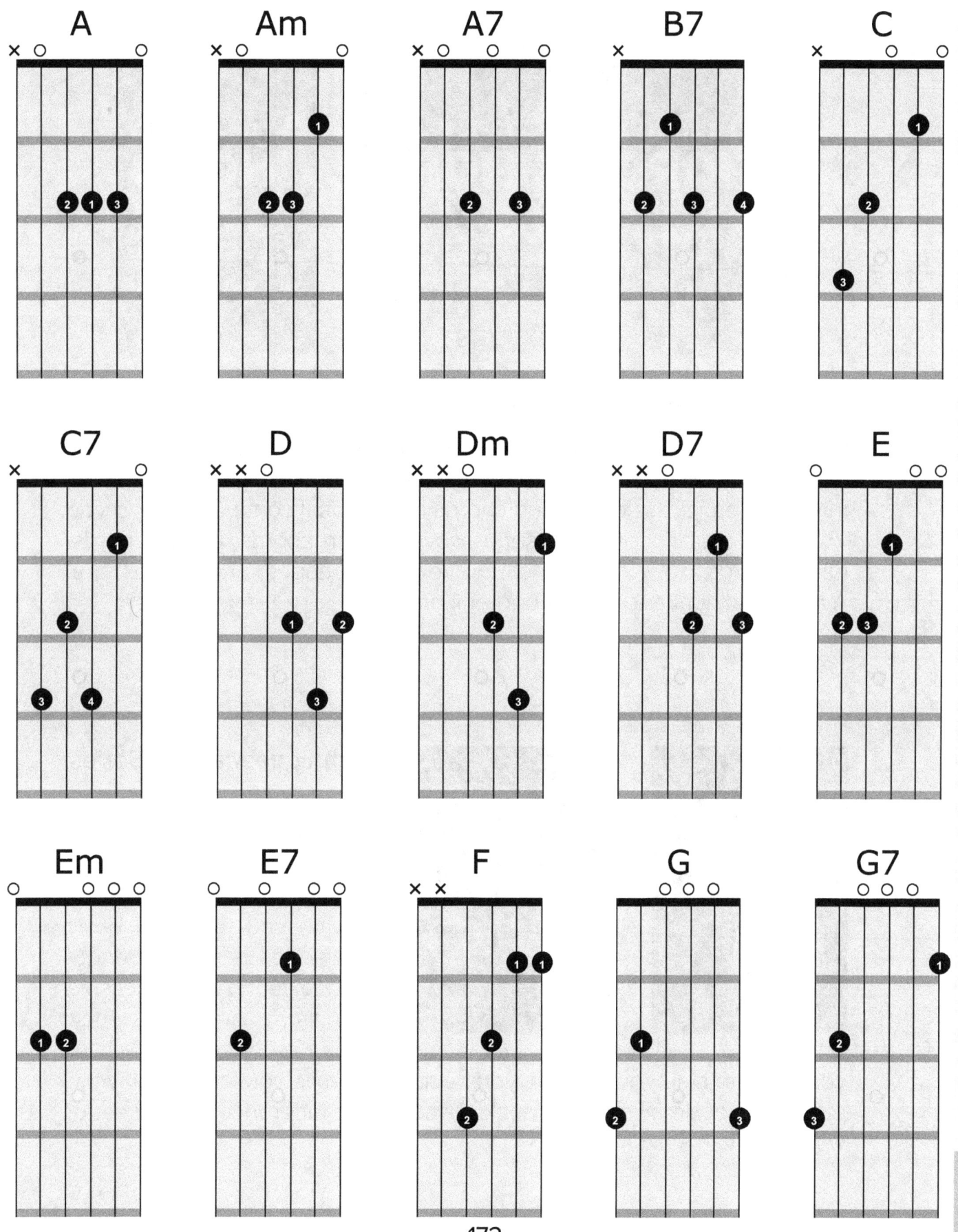

Resources to Take Your Playing Further

Guitar Chord Master™ Series

Guitar Chord Master is the only method book series that focuses exclusively on learning chords and strum patterns. Each book takes you step-by-step through the process of learning chords in a musical context, allowing you to master them for life! The series covers open chords, power chords, barre chords, how to use a capo, moveable shapes, and much more. Available in right and left-handed editions.

 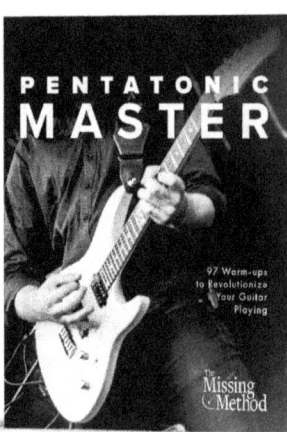

Technique Master™ Series

Avoid injury and learn how to play the right way with The Technique Master Series. Book 1 gets you started by helping you focus on basic techniques that build strength and dexterity, while focusing on time and efficiency. Book 2: Pentatonic Master continues to help you develop your technique while you learn to play the pentatonic scale all over the neck. Discover the difference a good set of warm-ups can make!

Perfect Practice: How to Zero in on Your Goals and Become a Better Guitar Player Faster

Rethink how you practice and stop practice burn-out. Learn the secrets to transforming your practice time into time well-spent. This book will help you to figure out how to identify and overcome the obstacles in your way by showing you what to practice and how to structure your time so you see results faster.

 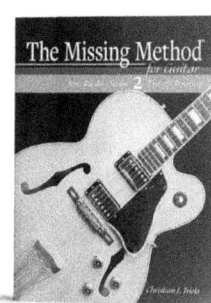   

The Missing Method for Guitar™ Note Reading Series

Unlock your musicianship with the power of note reading! The Missing Method for Guitar Note Reading Series teaches you how to read every note on the guitar, from the open strings to the 22nd fret. If you are looking to master the fretboard, this is the series for you! Available in right and left-handed editions.

Find these and more at TheMissingMethod.com.

Index

A

accidentals 81
acoustic guitar 4
action 7
active pickup 13
amps 10
  solid state amps 10
  tube amps 10
augmented fourth 150

B

bars 24
beat 24, 159, 168
bends
  bend and release 170
  grace note bend 170
  half-step bend 170
  pre-bend 170
  quarter-step bend 170
  whole-step bend 170
block chords 106
blues 130
bridge pickup 12

C

cables 11
capo 9
changing strings 166
chord, chords 28, 144, 153
  Am chord 36
  changing chords 27
  chord progression 39, 156
  chord symbols 28
  C major chord 36
  common chord progressions 39
  D7 chord 33
  dominant seven 28, 154
  Em chord 29, 30
  G major chord 29, 30
  major chord 28, 153
  major seventh 154
  minor chord 28, 154
  root 104, 153, 156
chord progression 39, 144, 156
  turnaround 157

chorus 41
classical guitar 5, 140
classical music 140
clef 54
country music 135
cowboy chords 135

D

dominant seven chord 28, 154
dotted half note 46
double-coil pickup 13
double stops 106

E

ear training 144
effect pedals 11
eighth notes 57, 160
eighth note strum 43
electric guitar 4

F

fingerstyle, fingerpicking 96
  P I M A 97
  P I M A M I 99
  P I M I A I M I 103
  Travis picking 104
flat, flats 81, 82
folk music 128
four-four time 45, 159

G

grace note bend 170
guitar
  amps 10
  cables 11
  capos 9
  caring for your guitar 22
  effect pedals 11
  parts diagram 6
  picks 9
  pickups 12
  practicing 20
  right hand technique 19
  string names 14

strings 8
string winder 166
strum technique 18
tuners 16
tuning 14
guitar tuners 16
guitar types 4
  acoustic guitar 4
  classical guitar 5
  electric guitar 4
  hollowbody electric 5

H

half note 24
half step 81
half-step bend 170
hammer on 171
hollowbody electric guitar 5
humbucker 13

I

improvisation 137
intervals 144, 145
  augmented fourth 150
  major second 149, 150
  major seventh 151
  major sixth 151, 152
  major third 148, 150
  minor second 149
  minor seventh 151
  minor sixth 151, 152
  minor third 148
  octave 146
  perfect fifth 147
  perfect fourth 147
  perfect intervals 147, 150
  tritone 150
  unison 146
intonation 7

J

jazz 137

L

lead 134

Index

A

accidentals 81
acoustic guitar 4
action 7
active pickup 13
amps 10
  solid state amps 10
  tube amps 10
augmented fourth 150

B

bars 24
beat 24, 159, 168
bends
  bend and release 170
  grace note bend 170
  half-step bend 170
  pre-bend 170
  quarter-step bend 170
  whole-step bend 170
block chords 106
blues 130
bridge pickup 12

C

cables 11
capo 9
changing strings 166
chord, chords 28, 144, 153
  Am chord 36
  changing chords 27
  chord progression 39, 156
  chord symbols 28
  C major chord 36
  common chord progressions 39
  D7 chord 33
  dominant seven 28, 154
  Em chord 29, 30
  G major chord 29, 30
  major chord 28, 153
  major seventh 154
  minor chord 28, 154
  root 104, 153, 156
chord progression 39, 144, 156
  turnaround 157

chorus 41
classical guitar 5, 140
classical music 140
clef 54
country music 135
cowboy chords 135

D

dominant seven chord 28, 154
dotted half note 46
double-coil pickup 13
double stops 106

E

ear training 144
effect pedals 11
eighth notes 57, 160
eighth note strum 43
electric guitar 4

F

fingerstyle, fingerpicking 96
  P I M A 97
  P I M A M I 99
  P I M I A I M I 103
  Travis picking 104
flat, flats 81, 82
folk music 128
four-four time 45, 159

G

grace note bend 170
guitar
  amps 10
  cables 11
  capos 9
  caring for your guitar 22
  effect pedals 11
  parts diagram 6
  picks 9
  pickups 12
  practicing 20
  right hand technique 19
  string names 14

strings 8
string winder 166
strum technique 18
tuners 16
tuning 14
guitar tuners 16
guitar types 4
  acoustic guitar 4
  classical guitar 5
  electric guitar 4
  hollowbody electric 5

H

half note 24
half step 81
half-step bend 170
hammer on 171
hollowbody electric guitar 5
humbucker 13

I

improvisation 137
intervals 144, 145
  augmented fourth 150
  major second 149, 150
  major seventh 151
  major sixth 151, 152
  major third 148, 150
  minor second 149
  minor seventh 151
  minor sixth 151, 152
  minor third 148
  octave 146
  perfect fifth 147
  perfect fourth 147
  perfect intervals 147, 150
  tritone 150
  unison 146
intonation 7

J

jazz 137

L

lead 134

    pull off 171
    quarter-step bend 170
    slides 171
    vibrato: 171
    whole-step bend 170
tablature, TAB 88
third 153
three-four time 45, 46, 159
tie 50
timbre 144
time 24, 56
    3/4 time 45
    4/4 time 24, 45
    bars 24
    beat 24
    dotted half note 46
    eighth note 57
    half note 24
    measure, measures 24
    meter 24
    quarter note 24
    rests 49
    rhythm 24
    whole note 24
Travis picking 104, 136
treble clef 54
triplets 160
tritone 150
tuners 16
tuning 14, 16
turnaround chord
      progression 157
twelve bar blues 40

U

unison 146

V

verse 41
vibrato: 171
visualization 27

W

whole note 24, 46
whole-step bend 170